Foreword

Liam Byrne, Minister for the Cabinet Office and
Kevin Brennan, Minister for the Third Sector

Government wants to strengthen the already powerful impact of third sector organisations in our economy. We are also leading a new drive to transform our public services.

While many third sector organisations have a powerful story to tell, the social and environmental value of the impact being made is often underplayed. As we face tough economic times, it is now more important than ever that we allow for better recognition of those who create social and environmental value, leading to more efficient movement of resources to the right people, in the right place, at the right time.

This new guide to Social Return on Investment is timely, as it will help third sector organisations to communicate better their impact to customers, government and the public, through measuring social and environmental value with confidence, in a standardised way that is easy for all to understand.

The guide should also underpin the thinking of commissioners and investors. For the public sector, it will help show us what really matters to the people who use public services and who benefit from third sector activity.

Ultimately, it is those in our communities in need of real help who will benefit.

Acknowledgements

This guide has been written by Jeremy Nicholls, Eilis Lawlor, Eva Neitzert and Tim Goodspeed, and edited by Sally Cupitt, with additional contributions from Sheila Durie, Jenni Inglis, Karl Leathem, Tris Lumley and Richard Piper.

Comments, guidance and advice were also received from the advisory group and from members of the SROI Network. Thanks to the following members of the SROI Network: Helen Fitzhugh, Adrian Henriques, Martin Kinsella, David Marshall, Kathleen Quinn, Kevin Robbie, Stephanie Robertson, Peter Scholten and Sara Williams.

Thanks to the following members of the advisory group: Saeeda Ahmed, Gustavo Bagattini, Simon Berry, Amitti CanagaRetna, Andrea Chauhan, Ken Cooper, Theresa Crawley, Elly de Decker, David Emerson, Tracy Houston, Pradeep Jethi, John Kingston, Martin Kinsella, Alan Knight, George Leahy, Liz Lloton Junoc, Joseph Lowe, Fergus Lyon, Claire Michelet, Ralph Mitchell, Penny Newman, Gerald Oppenheim, Akhil Patel, John Pearce, Tess Pendle, Matthew Pike, Martin Scott, Oliver Sian Davies, Richard Spencer, John Stewart, Chris Walker, Peter Wells and Jo Wheeler. Particular thanks also to Gustavo Bagattini and John Pearce.

A number of people and organisations have contributed to the development of SROI, started by Jed Emerson and the Roberts Enterprise Development Fund, developed by **nef** (the new economics foundation) and members of the SROI Network, and supported by, amongst others, the Hadley Trust, the Adventure Capital Fund and the Equal Social Economy Scotland Development Partnership.

Contents

Introduction

The Office of the Third Sector (OTS) and the Scottish Government recognise that demonstrating added social, economic and environmental value is important for third sector organisations and their funders, investors and commissioners, and is becoming increasingly important for the public and private sectors. The OTS has therefore funded a three-year programme on measuring social value. The work began in November 2008 and is being delivered by a consortium of organisations: the SROI Network, nef (the new economics foundation), Charities Evaluation Services, the National Council for Voluntary Organisations and New Philanthropy Capital.

In addition to this programme, the Scottish Government is also supporting SROI, including the development of a database of indicators to support SROI analysis.

This guide, which builds on the work in three earlier SROI guides[1], has been prepared as part of this programme. The purpose of this guide is to standardise practice, develop the methodology, and provide more clarity on the use of SROI. It has been written for people who want to measure and analyse the social, environmental and economic value being generated by their activities or by the activities they are funding or commissioning.

For more information on these programmes, and on other developments in SROI, please refer to the SROI Network website – www.thesroinetwork.org

---

1   *The SROI Framework*, drafted by Sara Olsen and Jeremy Nicholls; *A Guide to SROI Analysis* by Peter Scholten, Jeremy Nicholls, Sara Olsen and Brett Galimidi; and *Measuring Social Value*, by Eva Neitzert, Eilís Lawlor and Jeremy Nicholls (new economics foundation).

1 What is Social Return on Investment (SROI)?

Every day our actions and activities create and destroy value; they change the world around us. Although the value we create goes far beyond what can be captured in financial terms, this is, for the most part, the only type of value that is measured and accounted for. As a result, things that can be bought and sold take on a greater significance and many important things get left out. Decisions made like this may not be as good as they could be as they are based on incomplete information about full impacts.

Social Return on Investment (SROI) is a framework for measuring and accounting for this much broader concept of value; it seeks to reduce inequality and environmental degradation and improve wellbeing by incorporating social, environmental and economic costs and benefits.

SROI measures change in ways that are relevant to the people or organisations that experience or contribute to it. It tells the story of how change is being created by measuring social, environmental and economic outcomes and uses monetary values to represent them. This enables a ratio of benefits to costs to be calculated. For example, a ratio of 3:1 indicates that an investment of £1 delivers £3 of social value.

SROI is about value, rather than money. Money is simply a common unit and as such is a useful and widely accepted way of conveying value.

In the same way that a business plan contains much more information than the financial projections, SROI is much more than just a number. It is a story about change, on which to base decisions, that includes case studies and qualitative, quantitative and financial information.

An SROI analysis can take many different forms. It can encompass the social value generated by an entire organisation, or focus on just one specific aspect of the organisation's work. There are also a number of ways to organise the 'doing' of an SROI. It can be carried out largely as an in-house exercise or, alternatively, can be led by an external researcher.

There are two types of SROI:
- Evaluative, which is conducted retrospectively and based on actual outcomes that have already taken place.

- Forecast, which predicts how much social value will be created if the activities meet their intended outcomes.

Forecast SROIs are especially useful in the planning stages of an activity. They can help show how investment can maximise impact and are also useful for identifying what should be measured once the project is up and running.

A lack of good outcomes data is one of the main challenges when doing an SROI for the first time. To enable an evaluative SROI to be carried out, you will need data on outcomes, and a forecast SROI will provide the basis for a framework to capture outcomes. It is often preferable to start using SROI by forecasting what the social value may be, rather than evaluating what it was, as this ensures that you have the right data collection systems in place to perform a full analysis in the future.

The level of detail required will depend on the purpose of your SROI; a short analysis for internal purposes will be less time-consuming than a full report for an external audience that meets the requirements for verification.

The principles of SROI

SROI was developed from social accounting and cost-benefit analysis and is based on seven principles. These principles underpin how SROI should be applied and are set out in full in the Resources Section (page 80). The principles are:

- Involve stakeholders.

- Understand what changes.

- Value the things that matter.

- Only include what is material.

- Do not over-claim.

- Be transparent.

- Verify the result.

Judgement will be required throughout an SROI analysis. Often the principle of materiality will guide judgement, so this principle is very important. Materiality is a concept that is borrowed from accounting. In accounting terms, information is material if it has the potential to affect the readers' or stakeholders' decision. A piece of information is material if missing it out of the SROI would misrepresent the organisation's activities. For transparency, decisions about what is material should be documented to show why information has been included or excluded. At certain points we will indicate when it is useful to perform a materiality check. We encourage you to become familiar with the concept as it will inform your decisions throughout the process.[2]

The stages in SROI

Carrying out an SROI analysis involves six stages:

1 **Establishing scope and identifying key stakeholders.** It is important to have clear boundaries about what your SROI analysis will cover, who will be involved in the process and how.

2 **Mapping outcomes.** Through engaging with your stakeholders you will develop an impact map, or theory of change, which shows the relationship between inputs, outputs and outcomes.

---

2 Guidance from AccountAbility recommends that you consider the views of your stakeholders, societal norms, what your peers are doing, financial considerations, and organisational policies and objectives as criteria for judging materiality.

3 **Evidencing outcomes and giving them a value.** This stage involves finding data to show whether outcomes have happened and then valuing them.

4 **Establishing impact.** Having collected evidence on outcomes and monetised them, those aspects of change that would have happened anyway or are a result of other factors are eliminated from consideration.[3]

5 **Calculating the SROI.** This stage involves adding up all the benefits, subtracting any negatives and comparing the result to the investment. This is also where the sensitivity of the results can be tested.

6 **Reporting, using and embedding.** Easily forgotten, this vital last step involves sharing findings with stakeholders and responding to them, embedding good outcomes processes and verification of the report.

SROI has many similarities with other approaches and these are set out in the Resources section (page 80).

2 How SROI Can Help You

An SROI analysis can fulfil a range of purposes. It can be used as a tool for strategic planning and improving, for communicating impact and attracting investment, or for making investment decisions. It can help guide choices that managers face when deciding where they should spend time and money.

SROI can help you improve services by:
- facilitating strategic discussions and helping you understand and maximise the social value an activity creates;

- helping you target appropriate resources at managing unexpected outcomes, both positive and negative;

- demonstrating the importance of working with other organisations and people that have a contribution to make in creating change;

- identifying common ground between what an organisation wants to achieve and what its stakeholders want to achieve, helping to maximise social value;

- creating a formal dialogue with stakeholders that enables them to hold the service to account and involves them meaningfully in service design.

SROI can help make your organisation more sustainable by:
- raising your profile;

- improving your case for further funding;

- making your tenders more persuasive.

---

3   In the UK, HM Treasury maintains guidance on the methodology that should be used to make an economic assessment of the social costs and benefits of all new policies, projects and programmes. This guidance is set out in the *Green Book*. In the *Green Book* the idea of additionality is comparable with impact in SROI.

SROI is less useful when:

- a strategic planning process has already been undertaken and is already being implemented;

- stakeholders are not interested in the results;

- it is being undertaken only to prove the value of a service and there is no opportunity for changing the way things are done as a result of the analysis.

Comparing social return between different organisations

Organisations work with different stakeholders and will have made different judgements when analysing their social return. Consequently, it is not appropriate to compare the social return ratios alone. In the same way that investors need more than financial return information to make investment decisions, social investors will need to read all of the information produced as part of an SROI analysis. However, an organisation should compare changes in its own social return over time and examine the reasons for changes. Organisations should also endeavour to educate funders and investors on the importance of putting the ratio in the context of the overall analysis.

Certain situations require a different approach

This guide covers most situations. However, for situations where there is investment in assets, or the use of debt finance, there is a note in the Resources section (page 80).

3 Who Can Use SROI?

Types of organisation

SROI has been used by a range of organisations across the third, public and private sectors, including those that are small, large, new and established.

Third sector organisations and private businesses

Third sector organisations and private businesses that create social value can use SROI as a management tool to improve performance, inform expenditure and highlight added value. These may be start-up organisations developing business plans or established organisations. It can be used for analysing the value arising from trading activities whether the organisation is selling to the general public, to the public sector or to other businesses.

Commissioners and funders

Bodies that commission social value or invest in the creation of social value can use SROI initially as a way to help them decide where to invest, and later to assess performance and measure progress over time.

Both social investors and public service commissioners are in the business of securing social value that is delivered by third parties. The mechanisms by which that value is secured may differ but, by measuring that value, better decisions can be made. SROI can be used at three points in the commissioning or investment process:

- **Programme/pre-procurement** – forecast SROI analyses can be used at the strategic planning stage to decide how to set up a programme, for market testing and to determine scope and specification of contracts.

- **Application/bidding** – forecast SROI analyses can be used to assess which applicant or bidder is likely to create the most value. (Where applicants or bidders are already delivering the intervention that is being invested in, evaluative SROI can be used at the application/bidding stage.)

- **Monitoring and evaluation/contract management** – evaluative SROI analyses can be used to monitor the performance of a successful applicant or contractor.

Using SROI to inform public sector commissioning decisions is in line with HM Treasury guidance on value for money appraisals.[4] HM Treasury states that value for money assessments should be based on the 'optimum combination of whole-of-life costs and quality (or fitness for purpose) of the goods or service to meet the user's requirement'. These costs and benefits must include 'wider social and environmental costs and benefits for which there is no market price'.[5]

For developing policy
SROI can be used by organisations that develop public policy, for which recognition of social value is important. For example, it has been used to compare the value of investing in support-focused community penalties for women offenders as opposed to sending them to prison.[6]

Skills required to analyse the SROI report
Carrying out an SROI analysis requires a mixed set of skills. It will be helpful if you have prior experience of engaging stakeholders, outcomes measurement or evaluation, using Microsoft's Excel software and basic accounting skills. Even if you have experience in these areas, it may still be helpful to attend a training course. You can also bring in help from within your organisation, although, in the absence of this, you may need to arrange some external support.

Time requirement
Giving exact guidance on timescales is difficult because it is contingent on many factors, including scope, skills level and data availability, and whether you will be using the report for internal management or external reporting purposes.

All new measurement systems take some resources to implement. However, there are ways to keep the resources you require to a minimum. You could start with a project or contract rather than the whole organisation, or you could start with a forecast SROI analysis, especially when looking at a new business or a new activity. A forecast SROI analysis for internal management purposes, for example to help design information systems, would not need to be as detailed as a report you were planning on making public.

4   www.hm-treasury.gov.uk/data_greenbook_money_sustainability.htm
5   Further guidance on the use of SROI in public sector commissioning
    is available on the SROI Network website, www.thesroinetwork.org
6   *Unlocking value*, **nef**

An evaluative SROI analysis will be more time-consuming and could take several months, but the time required is much reduced if the organisation already produces good outcomes data or has a system of social accounting in place. However, it can take time to introduce systems to assess outcomes. Doing a forecast SROI analysis first can help one plan and prioritise the introduction of outcome assessment systems.

4 Using this Guide

This guide goes through the SROI process in stages. The completion of a table which maps out the analysis is central to the process. This table is called an Impact Map. There is a loose insert of the Impact Map included in the printed version of the guide, and copies are also available for download from the SROI Network website, www.thesroinetwork.org.

If you are new to SROI, please read the whole guide before starting. This is important because although it works through the process step by step, some of these steps can be completed at the same time, so reading the whole guide first may save you time later. Then return to the beginning and start working your way through. Bear in mind that not everything will be relevant to your analysis.

If you have some experience in SROI you may wish to use the guide as a reference tool. Social investors and commissioners interested in using SROI could focus on the introduction, the principles and the supplement on the SROI Network website, www.thesroinetwork.org.

Symbols
You will see these symbols throughout the guide:

Time for you to put what you have learned into practice. Over to you!

Top Tip: Alerts you to a top tip that can make life much easier for you.

The caution symbol warns you about common mistakes.

The return symbol highlights key points where you may decide you need to go back to an earlier step in the process.

It is important to remember that SROI is a framework based on principles. Often there are no right and wrong answers and you will need to use your judgement to respond to the question appropriately. The main points at which this is required are highlighted with this symbol.

 'Involve'. This symbol highlights points where you should involve your stakeholders to refine and confirm your decisions.

Language used

For simplicity we have used the following language throughout this guide:

- 'Social value' is used to describe social, economic and environmental value.

- 'The social return of your activity' is used rather than 'the social return of your organisation'. If you are analysing the social return of all your activities then this would be the same as the social return of your organisation.

- Where 'impact' is used we mean your outcomes after taking into account what would have happened anyway, the contribution of others and the length of time the outcomes last.

- The guide is written for 'you' although 'you' may be a single person or a team.

Wheels-to-Meals – The worked example

Throughout the guide we will use the fictional example of Wheels-to-Meals, which is presented in this format.

This is a hypothetical example. It is used to explore the principles and processes of SROI. Some elements of the impact map have been included to support learning and provide an appropriate example.

Wheels-to-Meals is a charity that developed from a meals on wheels service provided by volunteers. Increasingly, it realised that its clients not only needed the good hot meals it provided but, equally important, the contact and socialising with the volunteers who brought them.

Wheels-to-Meals provides a luncheon club to eligible elderly and disabled local residents and the majority of the volunteers are also elderly. The luncheon club is delivered with the same resources as a meals on wheels service, except that residents are transported to meals, rather than the other way round. The service includes provision of hot, nutritious lunches, transport, opportunities to socialise, and mild exercise. The service is available for up to 30 residents, 5 days a week and 50 weeks a year.

Resources available

There is a loose Impact Map enclosed in the printed version of this guide, which is also available for download from the SROI Network website, www.thesroinetwork.org. The Resources section on page 80 also includes:

- The format for an SROI report.

- A glossary.

- A note on cost allocation.

- A note on capital or loan-financed projects.

- Sources of support and further information.

- A summary of the relationship between SROI and other approaches.

- The seven principles of SROI.

- A checklist for SROI analysis – you can use this to tick off each step as you work through.

- An impact map for the worked example.

5   Future Updates

Like financial accounting and other ways of measuring, SROI is subject to further refinement and development. Users of this guide should check the website www.thesroinetwork.org for updates to the methodology.

Suggestions for changes can be made through the SROI Network website.

Stage 1:
Establishing scope and identifying stakeholders

Before you start your SROI analysis, you need to clarify what you are going to measure and how, and why you are embarking on a measurement process.

If you are carrying out an evaluative SROI analysis it may be useful to set up an SROI planning team. Winning management support at this early stage can help to make resources available for the SROI analysis, which in turn might allow you to extend its scope.

There are three steps in this stage:

1.1   Establishing scope
1.2   Identifying stakeholders
1.3   Deciding how to involve stakeholders

1.1 Establishing scope

The scope of an SROI analysis is an explicit statement about the boundary of what is being considered. It is often the result of negotiations about what is feasible for you to measure and what you would like to be able to improve or communicate. You will need to be clear about why you are conducting the analysis and what resources are available, and define the priorities for measurement. This stage will help ensure that what is being proposed is feasible.

The example below illustrates how a housing foundation made decisions about the scope of its SROI analysis.

Example: Establishing scope for a housing foundation
A large housing foundation was interested in calculating its social return to communicate its impact to its primary funder. The foundation has 35 employees and is involved in many activities, ranging from youth clubs to physical estate improvement projects. As there was no budget for the SROI analysis, it was decided that it would be conducted in-house and responsibility would rest with the quality manager at the foundation.

It was decided to publish the results of the SROI analysis alongside the end-of-year financial accounts in four months' time. The short timeframe, limited resources and the fact that the SROI analysis had to be completed in-house meant that the focus was to be on one project, with a plan to consider other projects in subsequent years. The decision was made to focus on a project which gave debt advice to tenants. This project has direct relevance for the foundation's primary funder, as one of the outcomes of the project is an increase in the number of tenants able to pay their rent.

What to consider in order to set scope
The issues you will need to consider include:

1 **Purpose**
   What is the purpose of this SROI analysis? Why do you want to begin this process now? Are there specific motivations driving the work, such as strategic planning or funding requirements?

2 **Audience**
   Who is this analysis for? This should cover an initial assessment of how you will communicate with your audiences.

3 **Background**
   Consider the aims and objectives of your organisation and how it is trying to make a difference. If you are focusing on specific activities you will need to understand the objectives of those activities. It is important that you have a clear understanding of what your organisation does and what it hopes to achieve by its activities. For sources of further support and information on this see the Resources section.

4 **Resources**
   What resources, such as staff time or money, will be required? Are these available?

5 Who will carry out the work?

Can you undertake the SROI analysis internally, or will you need to bring in external help? Make sure you have the right mix of skills and support from the start. Generally, you will need skills or experience in finance, accounting, evaluation and involving stakeholders.

6 The range of activities on which you will focus

Will you be analysing all the activities of your organisation, or just specific ones? You might want to separate the activities related to a particular source of funding,or those that are a priority for you. Keep your scope small if it is the first time you are doing an SROI analysis.

Clearly describe what you intend to measure. For example, if the activity was 'our work with young people', this may cover several departments within your organisation and you may actually mean something more specific, like 'mentoring support provided to young people'.

7 The period of time over which the intervention will be considered

SROI analysis is often annual, corresponding with annual financial accounting timescales. This can vary. For instance, a commissioner may want an evaluation of a specified timescale.

8 Whether the analysis is a forecast or an evaluation

If this is your first SROI report it will be much less time-consuming to prepare a forecast than to conduct an evaluative SROI analysis, unless you have the right outcomes data available. Otherwise, a forecast SROI analysis will help you to put in place a measurement framework so that you can come back to do evaluative SROI in the future.

Top Tip: Keep good records

Good record keeping is essential to successfully completing an SROI analysis. When you get to Stage 6, you will see that the SROI report needs to contain a lot more than just the calculation of the social return. It needs to document the decisions and assumptions you made along the way. Keeping a dedicated record of your planning and progress from the start will make writing the report a lot easier.

Adjusting the scope

Adjusting your scope in response to new information is good practice and not unusual. In particular, you may wish to review your scope after considering the numbers and types of stakeholders you need to involve. This will determine the resources required and it may mean you need to start with fewer activities.

The worked example – scope

Wheels-to-Meals is a charity that works with older people. Wheels-to-Meals provides transport for its members to come to a centre, where they are provided with hot, nutritious lunches. While at the centre, members have the opportunity to socialise, attend workshops on health and related issues, and take mild exercise.

The local authority contract for this charity is to become the subject of a joint commissioning approach. Wheels-to-Meals wants to contribute to the joint commissioning process with a credible demonstration of the social value it is creating. Wheels-to-Meals' staff and trustees worked together to define the scope of their upcoming SROI analysis and decided that it would:

- contribute to the joint commissioning process;
- cover all the activities of the organisation over one calendar year;
- be a forecast SROI analysis; and
- be undertaken by internal staff.

Remember that this is an example and is not intended to be a full analysis of scope.

Over to you: Establishing scope and constructing a plan
Consider these questions in relation to the SROI analysis you are undertaking.

1 What is the purpose of the SROI?

2 Who is it for?

3 What is the background?

4 What resources do you have available?

5 Who will undertake the SROI?

6 What activities will you focus on?

7 What timescale (period) will your analysis cover?

8 Is the analysis a forecast, a comparison against a forecast or an evaluation?

Record your answers, as you will need to refer to them during the analysis and when you come to write your report.

1.2 Identifying stakeholders

Listing stakeholders
Now that you are clear about the scope of the analysis, the next step is to identify and involve your stakeholders. **Stakeholders** are defined as people or organisations that experience change, whether positive or negative, as a result of the activity being analysed. In SROI analysis we are concerned primarily with finding out how much value has been created or destroyed and for whom.

To identify the stakeholders, list all those who might affect or be affected by the activities within your scope, whether the change or the outcome is positive or negative, intentional or unintentional.

The example below, which is referred to throughout the guide, relates to an organisation called MillRace IT. This is a real example as opposed to our worked example of Wheels-to-Meals. The example below shows you what a stakeholder list looks like.

Example: Listing stakeholders for MillRace IT
MillRace IT is a social firm offering supported volunteering and employment to people with mental health problems. At MillRace IT, computers are refurbished and distributed to new users, or serve as educational parts for the training programme.

Each year, some participants from MillRace IT move forward into employment after training. However, due to the nature of its core client base, some participants may never enter mainstream employment. In these cases, the goal is to provide a long-term volunteer opportunity, where clients are able to contribute and be productive in a supportive work environment. By spending time at MillRace IT, participants can avoid a relapse in their condition and extend their recovery.

MillRace IT is a former project of InterAct, another mental health charity, and the two organisations still work together. MillRace IT also has a commercial partnership with RDC, a private sector computer-recycling firm.

Here is a list of all those who affect or are affected by MillRace IT:

- Employees

- Individual customers who purchase recycled IT equipment

- Organisations which purchase IT services

- Members of the local community

- Project participants – people recovering from mental ill health

- The family members of project participants

- Local mental health care system

- InterAct, as the founding organisation

- RDC, the commercial company that offers office space to MillRace IT

- Local government

- National Health Service

- UK taxpayers

 Over to you: Draw up a list of your stakeholders

Deciding which stakeholders are relevant
You can see from the example above that the SROI process would quickly become unwieldy if you had to involve all possible stakeholders.

When deciding whether a stakeholder is relevant you need to think about what the outcomes may be for them. Which stakeholders are experiencing significant change as a result of your activities? In the next step you will be asking stakeholders about this from their perspective and this may mean you have to change your initial decision about the outcomes. However, at this stage you need an initial, broad understanding of stakeholder outcomes.

There is a tendency to focus on the positive outcomes that were intended (or expected) by your stakeholders, particularly if you focus only on your organisational aims or objectives, which do not usually identify unexpected or negative changes. However, intended and unintended outcomes and positive and negative outcomes are all relevant to SROI.

Some **unintended outcomes can be positive.** For example, a local economic development initiative undertook an evaluative SROI analysis and found that there had been a number of positive outcomes beyond getting a job. Those with children said they were now able to be better parents because getting a job had improved their general mental health and wellbeing. In some cases, unintended benefits can be more important to stakeholders than those that were intended.

However, **some unintended outcomes can be negative**. For example, a London-based charity flies young people from disadvantaged homes to Greece during the summer holidays, to give those children an educational experience and a holiday. Alongside the many positive outcomes for the young people, there is also an unintended negative consequence of carbon emissions from the flights. Including the carbon emissions simply makes the trade-off visible and might encourage ideas on how they achieve their objectives in a less carbon-intensive way.

One type of unintended change happens when your activity displaces someone else's activity. For example, reducing crime in one area may displace criminal activity to another area. In this case, the residents of the neighbouring area should be included as stakeholders. This may mean you need to reconsider your scope.

Top Tip: Unintended consequences and forecasting
If you are forecasting your return it may be more difficult for you and your stakeholders to assess possible unintended consequences. However, you may be able to use other people's previous experience of similar activities to identify unintended outcomes.

The example below continues with MillRace IT to show which stakeholders were included in the analysis and which were excluded. You will see that a reason is given for each decision, often based on a broad understanding of the outcomes for that stakeholder.

Example: Selecting material stakeholders at MillRace IT	
Key stakeholders	**Reason for inclusion**
Employees	Those employed would not otherwise be employed. This is a significant change to their lives
Project participants – people recovering from mental ill health	Primary beneficiaries who are likely to be experiencing significant outcomes if intervention is successful
The family members of project participants	Improvement in mental health of participants is likely to have a significant impact on families who may have previously had significant caring responsibilities
Local government in Essex	The computer recycling may reduce landfill charges for the local authority and help to meet environmental targets
National government (NHS and Department of Work and Pensions)	Savings in health spending if mental and physical health improves. Potential for reductions in benefit payments and increased state income from taxes where employment is increased
Excluded stakeholders	**Reason for exclusion**
Board members	No significant changes to board members were identified
Individual customers who purchase recycled IT equipment	Could buy computers elsewhere
Organisations that purchase IT services	Could buy services elsewhere
Members of the local community	Benefit likely to be too diffuse to measure in this analysis and difficulties in determining who would properly represent stakeholders in the community
Local mental health care system	Savings already captured by the national government (see above)

Make sure stakeholder outcomes link to your activities

Be careful that the stakeholders you have included experience change that is related to the activity in your scope. A common mistake is to include stakeholders that are relevant to the organisation but not to the activities set out in the scope. For example, if you are doing an SROI analysis of one project, be careful not to include stakeholders whose outcomes are achieved as a result of another project.

Make sure your choice of groups of stakeholders doesn't hide significant differences

When stakeholder groups are identified it is often assumed that they share enough common characteristics to form one group, for example 'local residents' or 'participants' or 'young people'. Yet members of these groups may experience and want different outcomes depending on their age, income or some other factor. If you think these differences are likely to be significant, split your stakeholders into subgroups.

Occasionally, you may find that past experiences have a major effect on whether participants achieve a particular outcome. For example, for an organisation working with young people, those who have previously had support from another organisation may do better when they work with you. Splitting them into subgroups now may help you sort out how much of the outcome was due to your intervention.

Over to you: Determining which stakeholders to include

Set up a table like the one below. Put all the stakeholders from your initial list in the first column, together with your initial assessment of how they affect or are affected by the activity, including positive and negative effects. Next decide which of the stakeholders experience significant change and are 'material' to the SROI analysis. Give your decision and a reason in the third column. Leave the remaining three columns blank until the next step.

Stakeholder and how they affect or are affected by the activity	What we think happens to them, positive and negative	Included/ excluded?	Method of involvement	How many?	When?

1.3 Deciding how to involve stakeholders

This section introduces you to methods of involving stakeholders. So far you have based your assessment of stakeholders and change on your own knowledge and experience.

As well as helping you find out what really matters to your stakeholders, involving them can help you to understand more about strengths and weaknesses of the activities you are analysing and may provide useful information that can help your organisation improve.

Methods for involving stakeholders

Collecting information from stakeholders can be as simple as phoning someone or as complex as holding a facilitated focus group session. When gathering information from participants, ask staff that work with them about the best way of engaging them. Here is a list of possible methods for involving stakeholders:

- Get stakeholders together in one place and ask them directly;

- Try a workshop format, with informal discussions and a flipchart to record responses;

- Have stakeholders complete a form during a regularly scheduled meeting – for example, an annual general meeting of an organisation, or other set gathering;

- Ring representatives from key stakeholder groups and ask them;

- Email a short form to representatives from key stakeholder groups;

- Have a social event and ask staff members to walk around and speak to stakeholders;

- One-to-one interviews.

Ideally, you should collect information directly from stakeholders. However, lack of time or resources may mean that some information has to come from existing research with your stakeholders. Where possible these existing sources should themselves be based on asking your stakeholders. Also, there may be stakeholders you cannot involve – future generations, for example. In this case you need to identify people to speak on their behalf.

Top Tip: Be practical about involving stakeholders
It is particularly important to be sensitive to the amount of time and resources stakeholders can give to this process, whether they are staff, funders, or participants. Think about each stakeholder's inputs, outputs and outcomes before meetings to ensure that time is used as efficiently as possible. If it is likely that you will have to speak to them again to collect more data for your analysis, make sure that you tell them this so they know what to expect.

Think about ways in which people already gather, for example public meetings or training sessions, and see if you can make use of any of these. Also, where you are asking people to give a significant amount of time to the process with no obvious benefit to them, consider providing incentives such as lunch, travel expenses or vouchers to encourage attendance.

How much involvement?

At this initial stage you do not have to worry about getting a large sample that is statistically representative. You can stop doing new research when you no longer 'hear' new things and so can reasonably expect to have heard the main points. This approach is commonly used in social research and is called 'saturation'.

Using time effectively

Involving your stakeholders need not be onerous or time-consuming and is often a way of checking and refining your work.[1] However, you can limit time spent on this by being creative.

By planning ahead you may be able to use your time (and that of your stakeholders) effectively by collecting data for several stages at once. So don't feel that you have to keep going back to your stakeholders.

For forecast SROI analyses you can often collect the information needed for stages 2, 3 and 4 in one session.

For evaluative SROI analyses you can collect information for stages 2 and 3.1 in one session – although you will need to collect the information in stage 3.2 as a separate exercise. As a result you may be able to collect the information you need for the remainder of stages 3 and 4 either in the first session or at the same time as you collect the information for stage 3.2.

Regardless of the type of SROI analysis, you will also need to engage with your stakeholders for stage 6.

Over to you: Planning for involving stakeholders

Now that key stakeholders have been identified, fill in the next three columns of the plan for involving stakeholders that you started in section 1.2. Put in the details of how you will involve them, how many you will involve and when. This plan will be summarised and form part of your report.

---

1   In HM Treasury's *Green Book* the principle of proportionality states that the amount of time spent on analysis should be proportionate to the amount being spent on the activity overall.

Stage 2:
Mapping outcomes

In this section we build an Impact Map informed by our engagement with stakeholders. This details how the activities you are analysing use certain resources (inputs) to deliver activities (measured as outputs) which result in outcomes for stakeholders. The Impact Map is central to the SROI analysis. Sometimes this relationship between inputs, outputs and outcomes is called a 'theory of change' or a logic model – or the story of how your intervention makes a difference in the world. You will gain the information from your stakeholders using the plan you established in the previous stage. By involving stakeholders in constructing the Impact Map you ensure that the outcomes that matter to those who are directly affected will get measured and valued.

Stage 2

There are five steps when filling out an Impact Map:

2.1   Starting on the Impact Map
2.2   Identifying inputs
2.3   Valuing inputs
2.4   Clarifying outputs
2.5   Describing outcomes

2.1 Starting on the Impact Map

A loose Impact Map has been included with the printed version of this guide. You can work with this or you could set up your own using Microsoft's Excel or Word software. A pdf of the Impact Map is also available at www.thesroinetwork.org.

The top section of the Impact Map is for information on your organisation and the scope of the analysis from your project plan. Below this, the first two columns of the bottom section ('stakeholders' and 'intended or unintended changes') are based on the stakeholder analysis completed in step 1.3. The last column on the Impact Map is for you to record things you need to do at a later point as you go along. Throughout this stage, the rest of the Impact Map is filled in step by step. We illustrate each step using the worked example.

Top Tip: Impact Maps

If this is the first time you have done an Impact Map it may be easier to work through all the exercises for inputs, outputs and outcomes in relation to one stakeholder and then repeat this for the next stakeholder.

The worked example – starting the Impact Map
Wheels-to-Meals' first step was to complete the top section of the Impact Map with scope and other details, as follows (to view in full, see pages 102 and 103):

Social Return on Investment – The Impact Map for the worked example		
Organisation	Wheels-to-Meals	
Objectives	Provide luncheon club for 30 elderly local residents with additional health and social benefits by bringing residents to meals	
Scope	Activity	30 places for eligible elderly and/or disabled local residents 5 days a week, 50 weeks of the year
	Contract/Funding/Part of organisation	Local Authority Grant

The second step was to fill out the first two columns. Look at the Impact Map for Wheels-to-Meals on page 102: the orange section shows you how these columns have been completed.

Wheels-to-Meals considered the stakeholders that have an effect on its activity and on whom the activity has an effect. However, it decided not to include them all. For example, the local primary care trust could have been a stakeholder but was not included because a number of other significant stakeholders had been identified and there were insufficient resources to analyse more stakeholders for a relatively small activity.

Over to you: Starting on the Impact Map
Fill in the top section and first two columns of your Impact Map.

2.2 Identifying inputs

The inputs column is the next one to fill in on your Impact Map. The investment, in SROI, refers to the financial value of the inputs. You need to able to identify what stakeholders are contributing in order to make the activity possible – these are their inputs. Inputs are used up in the course of the activity – money or time, for example.

The value of the financial inputs, especially for a single grant or a contract, is usually easy to establish, although it is important that you include the full cost of delivering the services. In some situations there are other contributions being made, including non-cash items, which need to be valued. Further information on valuing non-cash inputs is available in the Resources section (see index on page 81).

Where you are analysing the social value generated by an activity that is financed from several sources, some initial analysis of the costs of these activities is required and there is specific guidance on this in the Resources section (see index on page 81).

Beware of double counting inputs
Be careful that all the inputs you record are used in delivering the activity. Your organisation may not use all the funding for an activity; this 'surplus' relates to the amount of the finance that was not necessary for the activity to happen. If there is a surplus then a different treatment is required: either you should include the additional social value that would be generated if you spent the surplus, or you should reduce the value of the input by the amount of the surplus.

2.3 Valuing inputs

When filling out your Impact Map you may have identified non-monetised inputs; these are inputs other than the financial investment, like volunteer time. If the activity would not go ahead to the same extent without these inputs, then you will want to put a value on them. This will ensure that you are transparent about the full cost of delivering your service. This section is for those that want to give a value to their non-monetised inputs.

Two main types of non-monetised inputs are generally relevant in SROI: volunteer time and contributions of goods and services in kind. Valuing volunteer time can be more difficult.

The hours given by volunteers are often given a value equivalent to the average hourly rate for the type of work they are doing. For example, if an administration volunteer does 5 hours a week in an area where administration work is paid on average £5 per hour, their weekly input would be £25. This value is given regardless of whether any money is paid to the volunteer; it simply gives the input a value that can be added up with other inputs.

Volunteer inputs can also include an allocation of the overheads that would be incurred if the person was employed. This would cover National Insurance and pension contributions and also the costs of desk space, electricity, and so on.

The current convention in SROI is that the time spent by the beneficiaries on a programme is not given a financial value.[2]

Forecasting SROI

If you are forecasting your social return, the quantity of inputs that will be required will be an estimate based on a mix of:

- your experience;

- data from previous years' activity – if you have it; and/or

- research based on other people's experience of the levels of inputs you may require.

Evaluating SROI

If you are evaluating your social return, you will want to obtain the information from your organisation's management systems, such as records of how many hours or days your volunteers contributed. If this is not available, then you can use an estimate for now and this will be an action point for the future.

The worked example – inputs
Look at the Impact Map for Wheels-to-Meals on page 102: the pink section shows you how the column for inputs has been completed.

The material inputs for the scope and stakeholders are primarily time and money. In this example volunteer time is valued at £6/hr – an estimate of minimum wage for 2010 (the end of the period of the forecast). There are different ways of valuing volunteer time depending on the work being done by the volunteers. In this case, the value used is in line with volunteering England's (www.volunteering.org.uk) figure for a kitchen and catering assistant.

Over to you: Inputs
Once you have asked your stakeholders about inputs, fill in the inputs column on your impact map. Where required, try to attach a value.

2.4 Clarifying outputs

Outputs are a quantitative summary of an activity. For example, the activity is 'we provide training' and the output is 'we trained 50 people to NVQ level 3'. You can work through your list of stakeholders, describing the outputs from the activity.

2   This is currently under discussion within the SROI Network.

Sometimes the same output is repeated for several stakeholders, which are included in SROI at this stage because they form part of the theory of change. They will not be counted in the calculation, so there is no risk of double counting. In situations where stakeholders are contributing their time, the output – a number of hours – may be described in the same way as the inputs: a number of hours.

The worked example – outputs
Look at the Impact Map for Wheels-to-Meals on page 102: the pink section shows you how the column for outputs has been completed.

The activity, in this example, is the same for all stakeholders – the luncheon club. However, it needed to be broken down into outputs. So, 'luncheon club' is an important part of the story and context, but the impact map also quantifies the outputs: group activities, transport and meals.

Over to you: Outputs
Once you have asked your stakeholders about outputs, fill in the outputs column on your Impact Map.

2.5 Describing outcomes

Outcomes for stakeholders
SROI is an outcomes-based measurement tool, as measuring outcomes is the only way you can be sure that changes for stakeholders are taking place. Be careful not to confuse outputs with outcomes. For example, if a training programme aims to get people into jobs then completion of the training itself is an output, getting the job is an outcome. Identifying outcomes is not always immediately intuitive, be sure to spend sufficient time getting to grips with the theory of change to ensure that you are measuring the right things.

You have already set out your view of the intended or unintended outcomes that you expect. Now you need to check with your stakeholders to see if this view was correct. They may describe the effects differently to you, perhaps even in surprising ways. You may find that you need to include a new stakeholder. For this reason, the outcomes description column can only be completed after talking to your stakeholders. It can help identify outcomes if you ask stakeholders some questions. For example: 'How would you describe how your life has changed?; 'What do you do differently now?'.

Remember that this symbol appears throughout the guide but that you may be able to collect information from stakeholders relating to several stages at the same time (see page 26).

Relate outcomes to the right stakeholder
Don't write down outcomes against one stakeholder that relate to changes that happened to another stakeholder. For example, if in step 1.3 you recorded

the 'increased integration of refugees' as an intended change for your funder, you need to recognise that this is really an outcome for refugees. If this is also recorded as an outcome against the funder it would be double counting. Sometimes, although a stakeholder contributes to the activity, they are not significantly changed by it.

In cases where the state is the funder there may be changes to society which you could include. In the above example, integration of refugees may reduce benefit payments which can then be included as a change for the state.

Stage 2

Making a judgement on outcomes

In deciding on outcomes, you should consider other factors, such as the organisation's objectives, as well as the views of your stakeholders. Stakeholders' views are critical but they are not the only factors in deciding which outcomes are significant. SROI is described as stakeholder-informed, rather than stakeholder-led, to recognise this.

This has some practical implications. For example, a substance user may express a desire to continue using. In these cases you may decide not to include the desired outcomes of one of your stakeholders as they conflict with your organisation's own intended outcomes and values.

Top Tip: Soft and hard outcomes
People sometimes use the terms 'soft' outcomes and 'hard' outcomes – the latter being outcomes that are easier to measure or subject to more established means of measurement. It is better to avoid this categorisation because if a 'soft outcome' is significant to the stakeholders it will need to be included in your SROI analysis, so it will be necessary to find a way to measure it.

Intermediate outcomes, or distance travelled

Sometimes it takes years for outcomes to take place – for example, slowing the rate of climate change – but there may be observable changes along the way. You may have heard this described as distance travelled, intermediate outcomes, or a chain of events. It is important to establish what this chain of events is, not least because your activity may only bring about some changes in the chain.

When a new outcome is identified by stakeholders or by your assessment of other factors, you will need to decide whether it is an entirely new outcome, or in fact part of an existing chain of events.

The worked example – describing outcomes

Look at the Impact Map for Wheels-to-Meals on page 102, the pink section shows you how the column for describing outcomes has been completed.

the initial analysis was undertaken, one of the assumptions was that residents would be healthier. However, during initial discussions with stakeholders, it soon became clear that for many residents this was not where the story ended. As a result of exercise sessions, residents were fitter. This resulted in a reduction in falls. Several residents said things like, "Well, I don't end up in hospital as much for a start!" when they were asked what they thought happened to them as a result of coming to the luncheon club. This outcome had not been identified as significant before but it appeared to be an important part of the story for many of this stakeholder group.

To understand this, Wheels-to-Meals considered the 'chain of events' that was occurring as a result of the outputs. So, for this example of fewer falls, the chain of events was:

Activity	Example output	Outcome 1	Outcome 2	Outcome 3
Luncheon club	group activities, including exercise sessions	as a result residents were fitter	as a result they fell less	as a result they ended up in hospital less

These three outcomes are all describing different stages of one change.
The activity and output(s) are summarised together in the outputs column.
The outcomes are summarised together in the outcomes description column.

By involving stakeholders, Wheels-to-Meals also identified an important unintended negative outcome – by coming to the luncheon club, some residents were no longer being supported by neighbours who had been popping in and doing shopping for them. Neighbours were a new stakeholder group, so a new row was included in the Impact Map and inputs, outputs and outcomes for this group were recorded.

In exploring a chain of events, you may notice that there are different chains for different groups of people within a single stakeholder group. Where this happens you may feel that the differences are significant and you may need to split a stakeholder group into one or more groups, each with a different chain.

Over to you: Finalising what to measure
Once you have asked your stakeholders about outcomes and considered other factors, fill in the outcomes column on your impact map. This chain of events is often described as a theory of change. You can write up the theory of change for each stakeholder and the relationship to the activity covered in your scope. This will form part of your report.

This is also a useful point at which to check your Impact Map to make sure you have only included material outcomes and make any appropriate revisions. Check that you aren't missing anything significant or including something that is not relevant. Take a moment to look at your Impact Map and decide what you will finally include before moving on to measurement. If you make a decision to exclude any outcomes, make sure you document this, and the reasons why, in your SROI report.

Stage 3:
Evidencing outcomes and giving them a value

So far you have mapped out and described the outcomes that are occurring for stakeholders. In this step, we develop outcome indicators and use these to collect evidence on the outcome that is occurring.

There are four steps in stage 3:

3.1   Developing outcome indicators
3.2   Collecting outcomes data
3.3   Establishing how long outcomes last
3.4   Putting a value on the outcome

3.1 Developing outcome indicators

Indicators are ways of knowing that change has happened. In SROI they are applied to outcomes as these are the measures of change that we are interested in.

The next stage in developing the impact map is to clarify one or more indicators for each of the outcomes on your map. You will need indicators that can tell you both whether the outcome has occurred, and by how much.

Time to involve your stakeholders
Stakeholders are often the best people to help you identify indicators, so ask them how they know that change has happened for them.

For example, if the outcome was an increase in self-confidence, ask the people whose self-confidence is increased what they now do as a result, or ask them to tell you what they mean by self-confidence. In this way you are more likely to get to something that you can measure. They might say: "Before [the activity] I would never go out, but now I get the bus into town to meet my friends." In this example the indicator of self-confidence could be whether people go out more or spend more time with other people.

Balancing subjective and objective indicators
Sometimes you need to use more than one indicator. Try to mix subjective (or self-reported) and objective indicators that complement each other. There are risks of relying on self-reporting measures that can be offset by supporting them with objective indicators. Check your indicators with your stakeholders. For example, frequency of use of GP services is commonly used to measure health outcomes but could be either positive or negative depending on the circumstances (eg increased use of GP services is often a positive outcome for homeless people who are less likely to present with health problems when they arise).

The example below is for a mental health day service.

Example: Choosing indicators	
Outcome	Indicator
Reduced social isolation	• Whether participants are taking part in new activities (eg taking up new sports or hobbies, visiting new places) • Whether participants report having more friends • Level of social skills reported by participants • Whether participants are accessing relevant public services that they had not used in the past, like public transport
Decreased stigmatisation of people with mental health problems	• Number of activities participants are involved in outside the mental health services • Number of incidents of discrimination reported by participants • Involvement of local community in organisation's activities • Change in attitudes within the local community

The worked example – indicators

Look at the Impact Map for Wheels-to-Meals on page 103: the blue section shows you how the columns for indicators has been completed.

The indicators for some outcomes were quite straightforward. For example, the outcome 'fewer hospital admissions' has a simple indicator: number of hospital admissions.

In other cases – healthier residents, for example – indicators needed to be identified to measure the outcome described. In this case, Wheels-to-Meals chose an objective indicator ('fewer GP visits') and a subjective indicator ('number of residents reporting improved health'). The subjective and objective indicators support each other.

Checking your indicators

Now that you have indicators that are relevant to the stakeholder and scope, you need to check that they are not only measurable but that you will be able to measure them within the scope and the resources you have set.

If you are completing a forecast SROI report you need to check that you could reasonably measure your indicators in future. If you are doing an evaluative SROI analysis, you need to check the cost of collecting information about outcomes that have happened, if the information is not available. This can be expensive as it can involve surveys of people who are no longer involved with your organisation. If, for example, a survey is not possible, one of the recommendations is likely to be to change the way you capture information in future.

Sometimes your stakeholder will only achieve the outcome they seek later on, when they are no longer working with you. You will need to maintain contact with your stakeholders to make sure you capture this and that you therefore have indicators that are relevant to your stakeholders. This can be done through postal and telephone surveys and can be limited to a representative sample. You may need to provide a financial incentive for your stakeholders to respond.

Measure what matters

A common mistake here is to misinterpret what we mean by measurable. A basic principle of SROI is to measure and value the things that matter. Measurability means expressing the outcome indicator in terms that are measurable, rather than finding an indicator that is easy to measure.

Avoid the trap of using inappropriate indicators just because they are readily available. If the outcome is important you will need to find a way to measure it.

Top Tip: Knowing the numbers
In an Impact Map, indicators are often expressed using terms like 'more', 'fewer', 'less' or 'increased' – such as 'a 20% decrease in school exclusions'. Strictly speaking the indicator is 'number of exclusions'. In order to know whether the number of exclusions has changed you will need to know the actual numbers of exclusions before and after the activity.

Over to you: Choosing indicators
Return to your Impact Map. For each outcome, choose indicators that will tell you whether the outcome has occurred, and to what extent. Try to think of more than one indicator per outcome to strengthen your findings and help you be sure that the outcome has occurred.

3.2 Collecting outcomes data

You will now need to collect data on your indicators. This may be available from existing sources (internal or external) or you may need to collect new data.

If you are doing a forecast SROI analysis, use existing data where available. If you have delivered this activity before, you can base your estimation on your own previous experience. If this is the first time you have undertaken the activity, then your estimate will be based on research or other people's experience in similar activities. Look at information from:

- Membership organisations, government departments, market research firms, consulting companies, partner organisations; and

- Published research from universities, government departments and research organisations.

As part of your forecast SROI analysis, it is important to change the way you collect data so that you have the right information in place to carry out an evaluative SROI study at a later date. Think about ways that you can incorporate this into everyday activities to make it as cost-effective as possible. For example, a childcare intervention could engage with parents at regular intervals as they collect their children and record outcomes that way.

If you are doing an evaluative SROI analysis, use and review the data the organisation already collects and what is available from other sources. It is more time-consuming and costly to gather data about impact after the event, and existing data and self-reported change may have to suffice.

New data will usually come from people directly involved in the creation of social value – project participants or employees, for example – and will be gathered by your organisation. You may be able to get another organisation, like the local authority, to agree to let you include questions in a standard questionnaire that it would administer.

The most commonly used techniques for primary data collection include:

- One-to-one interviews

- Record keeping (such as case files)

- Focus groups

- Workshops and seminars

- Questionnaires (face-to-face, over the phone, in the post, on the Internet).

A common question is how big the sample of your clients should be. There is no hard and fast rule here. If you work with twenty young people, you should try and speak to all of them. If you work with thousands of people, you should use a representative sample and statistical tests to support your arguments. If this is not feasible it is recommended that you choose a sample size that you feel is defensible and within your budget. See the sources of further information in the Resources section (page 80) for help in calculating sample sizes and for drawing conclusions from samples.

Finding relevant data can be difficult, so use the best available information or make assumptions or estimates. Do not worry about not being able to collect every piece of data. You may even conclude that it would be best to go back to Stage 1 and redefine your scope until more resources are available and organisational priorities permit. Remember that in order to be transparent you will need to explain what you have used. The table below gives you some examples of collecting outcomes data for a community-based employment-mentoring programme.

Stakeholder	Outcome	Indicator	Data Collection
Unemployed person	Gains and maintains employment	Whether in work after 12 months	Annual postal survey of stakeholders and telephone follow up
Participant with physical disability	Reduced social isolation	Frequency of social contact with friends	Gathered systematically at six month review between client and worker
Young person	Improved behaviour	Number and type of school exclusions	Report by teacher
Local authority	Increase in recycling	Amount of waste going to landfill	Monitoring of change in amount of waste
Local community	Reduced fear of crime	Number of local people who report feeling safer	Home Office crime mapping tool

Top Tip: Tap into innovation on outcomes measurement
Sometimes you will find that there is an indicator but there is currently no way
of measuring it and new methods need to be developed[1]. It was once commonly
thought that confidence, self-esteem and other experiential outcomes could not be
measured. However, there are many techniques for measuring a range of wellbeing
outcomes that are now widely accepted by government and charities.
Look into what is already being done in this area that could be used or adapted for
your purposes, or consider how you can work with others to develop new ways of
measuring outcomes.

Local Multiplier (LM3) is an example of a tool that was developed by **nef** in
order to measure local money flows. See www.procurementcupboard.org for
more information. A tool called the Outcomes Star has been developed to assist
homelessness charities to capture the distance travelled by their clients. This is a
good example of how you can measure progress towards an outcome. You can find
more information about the Outcomes Star at www.homelessoutcomes.org.uk

Worked example – source and quantity of indicators
Look at the Impact Map for Wheels-to-Meals on page 103: the blue section shows
you the source and quantity of the indicators.

Do not double count outcomes
When you are dealing with a chain of events, be careful not to double count.
For example: ten people want to gain work through training and all ten gain
qualifications. But only five gain work. When you come to value the outcome for
the five that gained work, valuing both the qualification and the employment will
double count the value of the training.

Another situation where there is a risk of double counting is when looking at
savings to the state. For example, an SROI study might include the financial
saving to the state of reducing homelessness. However, such calculations can
include savings to the NHS on healthcare. You shouldn't then separately include
the savings to the NHS as it would be double counting. But remember this is
subtle. For example, if a disabled person gets a job, benefits might accrue to
them (expressed in part through income), to their carer (respite), and to the state
(tax and benefits). Counting all three is not considered double counting in SROI
because the value is experienced separately by all three stakeholders.

To distinguish between the two, ask yourself: am I counting the same value, for
the same stakeholder, twice?

---

1   Go to www.thesroinetwork.org for information on the indicator database.

Over to you: Outcomes data collection

Complete the column on the Impact Map for sources of information. Once you've collected your data, fill in the 'quantity' column.

Don't forget that you are communicating to different audiences and may need a number of different types of information. Almost always it will help people understand what you do and explain how you create change if you can record short case studies of one or two people or organisations in each stakeholder group. These would form part of a full SROI report. You should now have enough information to be able to prepare these.

3.3 Establishing how long outcomes last

The effect of some outcomes will last longer than others. Some outcomes depend on the activity continuing and some do not. For example, in helping someone to start a business it is reasonable to expect the business to last for some time after your intervention. Conversely, providing a service so that people do not visit their GP so often may depend on the service being available all the time.

Where you believe that the outcome will last after the activity has stopped, then it will also continue to generate value. The timescale used is generally the number of years you expect the benefit to endure after your intervention. This is referred to as the duration of the outcome or the benefit period.

You will need an estimate of the duration of each of your outcomes. Ideally this would be determined by asking people how long an intervention lasted for them – this will give you evidence of the duration. However, if information is not available on the durability of different outcomes, you can use other research for a similar group to predict the benefit period, such as the likelihood that ex-offenders will begin offending again, or that people in employment will lose their jobs. Look for research to support your decision. It is important to use data that is as close as possible to the intervention in question so as not to inappropriately generalise. This is an area where there can be a tendency to overstate your case and lose credibility.

Sometimes the duration of the outcome is just one year and it only lasts while the intervention is occurring. In other instances it might be 10 or even 15 years. For example, a parenting intervention with children from deprived areas may potentially have effects that last into adulthood. You will need to have longitudinal data to support the duration of the outcome and should consider how you might start to collect this (if you are not already doing so). If you don't have this information you will need to make a case based on other research. The longer the duration, the more likely it is that the outcome will be affected by other factors, and the less credible your claim that the outcome is down to you. This is addressed by looking at the rate at which the outcome drops off and is considered in Step 4.4.

Beneficiaries	Duration	Rationale
Participants on a year-long IT training programme that go on to get related employment	4–5 years	The move into successful employment could set participants on a career path. Although they might stay on this for some time (eg 15 years), the period is kept to 4-5 years as increasingly the effect of the training will wear off and their work experience will become more important
Carers that get brief respite (1 week)	Up to 1 year	Respite care needs to be regular in order to sustain the benefits
Children that get a preschool intervention.	10–15 years	Evidence from some other early interventions with children suggests that the benefit can be long lasting, setting children on a different path
Businesses that get support with cheap workspace	3–4 years	The support could set up businesses that last for much longer than 3-4 years. However, it is likely that after the initial set up other factors (eg the general economic climate) will become more important
Participants that get better-quality wheelchairs	2 years	The benefit of the new wheelchair will depreciate much like other assets

Duration and life expectancy are different

In the case of capital projects it is important to recognise the difference between the duration of the benefit and the life expectancy of the asset. For example, a new building may last 20 years and in each year create benefits which last several years. There is a note in the Resources section on using SROI with capital projects.

Keep a record of the rationale you used for determining the benefit period for each outcome. This will need to go into your SROI report.

To date, the convention in SROI has been to account for outcomes from the time period after the activity, even if they occur during the activity.[2]

The worked example – duration

Look at the Impact Map for Wheels-to-Meals on page 103: the blue section shows you how the column for the duration of the outcome has been completed.

For Wheels-to-Meals, most of the benefit occurs during the activity and would not be sustained if the luncheon club ceased to operate. However, in line with convention,

2   This is a simplification of the approach used in HM Treasury's *Green Book*, where the outcomes are accounted for in the time period they arise. There is a risk that the simplification used in SROI will distort the calculation of social value in some situations. Although SROI uses this simplification, it is perfectly possible to calculate the SROI based on the time periods in which the outcomes occur, in which case it is important to state that this is what has been done.

this is accounted for as if it happened in the period after the activity. We will consider two examples: fewer falls as a result of the mild exercise and fewer GP visits as a result of the practice nurse sessions.

- Fewer falls
  The activities were designed to maintain and improve general wellbeing in older and less mobile people. We have assumed that residents would not have mild exercise sessions without coming to the luncheon club and so, for our impact map, residents will stop having these sessions at the end of the year and the benefit will not endure. The duration is one year.

- Fewer GP visits
  Here, the change is due to increased awareness of health issues and contributing factors. Residents are given knowledge. When they stop having the practice nurse sessions at the luncheon club they do not lose the knowledge. They might use it less as time goes on (the effect of which on our analysis is picked up later in "drop-off"), but the change is not reversed. So the benefit endures beyond the activity. We have estimated the duration to be 5 years.

Over to you: Duration of outcomes
Complete the 'Duration' column on your Impact Map.

3.4 Putting a value on the outcome

Now that you have quantities of each outcome indicator the next step is to give each outcome a financial value. Remember that you are identifying a value for the outcome and not the indicator. You will then be able to complete the columns on the impact map relating to financial proxies, their value and their sources.

What is valuation?
This process of valuation is often referred to as monetisation because we assign a monetary value to things that do not have a market price. All the prices that we use in our day-to-day lives are approximations – 'proxies' – for the value that the buyer and the seller gain and lose in the transaction. The value that we get will be different for different people in different situations.

For some things, like a pint of milk, there is considerable agreement on and consistency in the price. For other things, such as a house, there is likely to be a wider spread of possible prices. For others – a new product that has never been sold before, for example – there may be no comparison.

All value is, in the end, subjective. Markets have developed, in large part, to mediate between people's different subjective perceptions of what things are worth. In some cases this is more obvious than in others. But even where prices are stable ar the semblance of 'objective' or 'true' value, this is not really the case.

If we take the house example again, how much it is worth depends who we are referring to. If you are selling a house, you will have a sense of what you are prepared to accept for it – how much value it has for you. If I am thinking of buying your house, I have my own view of what I am prepared to pay – how much value it has for me. What the market does – in fact, what it is effectively for – is to bring together people whose valuations happen to coincide. This 'coincidence' is called 'price discovery' – but it is not uncovering any 'true' or 'fundamental' value, rather it is matching people who (broadly) agree on what something is worth.

Arriving at an estimate of social value is the same as this in almost every way. The difference is that goods are not traded in the market and so there is no process of 'price discovery'. This does not mean, however, that these social 'goods' do not have a value to people. If I want to buy a house but there are no sellers, this does not mean that it does not have a value to me or that I don't have an idea of what this is. Similarly, if a local authority creates a park for residents, where I can go, this too has a value to me. The fact that I have not had to pay for this does not negate this fact.

In SROI we use financial proxies to estimate the social value of non-traded goods to different stakeholders. Just as two people may disagree on the value of a traded good (and so decide not to trade), different stakeholders will have different perceptions of the value they get from different things. By estimating this value through the use of financial proxies, and combining these valuations, we arrive at an estimate of the total social value created by an intervention.

This is no different in principle to valuations on a stock market, which are simply a reflection of the cumulative subjective valuations of buyers and sellers. With SROI, however, the total valuation arrived at is likely to be more complete. Why? Because share prices only reflect the valuations of a very limited group of stakeholders (institutional and retail investors), while an SROI analysis, if done properly, captures the different types of value relating to an activity, intervention or organisation, as seen from the perspective of those that are affected – ie the stakeholders.

The process of valuation has a long tradition in environmental and health economics; SROI is building on the methodology and extending it to other fields. While it may seem initially daunting, it is relatively straightforward and gets easier with practice. As SROI becomes more widespread, monetisation will improve and there will be scope for pooling good financial proxies. Now we will take you through some guidance drawn from different disciplines for identifying proxies for each of these.

Proxies that are easy to source
Sometimes monetisation is a fairly straightforward process – where it relates to a cost saving, for example. This might be the case where you are interested in the value of improved health from the state's perspective; you may decide to use the cost of attending a GP clinic.

Sometimes this will not result in an actual cost saving because the scale of the intervention is too small to affect the cost in a significant way (see section on marginal ...sts, below) but it still has a value.

The flipside to cost savings is an increase in income. Rises in income for people through salary or for the state through tax increases are obvious examples. However, be careful of double counting here. For example, if an individual gets a job, they increase their income and the state receives increased taxes. In this case the increase in income should be recorded after deducting taxes.

The increase in income may also not be additional to either the person or the state. For the person the increased income may be offset by an increase in taxes or loss of benefits. For the state the increase in taxes will only result in an increase in government income if no one else loses work and the total level of employment increases. However, there may still be a value to the state of that person getting a job that should be included – perhaps because inequality has been reduced.

Remember we are talking about proxies here, as some of these outcomes will not result in actual financial savings. However, for some stakeholders, such as the funders, you may want to demonstrate cash savings. If you want to do this credibly you will need to approach it rigorously and should consult the guidance on marginal costs and displacement. The information you collect on costs will help you with this but it may require a separate calculation.

Proxies that are more challenging

SROI also gives values to things that are harder to value so are routinely left out of traditional economic appraisal. There are several techniques available.

In **Contingent valuation** we ask people directly how they value things. This approach assesses people's willingness to pay, or accept compensation, for a hypothetical thing. For example, you may ask people to value a decrease in aircraft noise in their town – their willingness to pay for it. Conversely, you may ask them how much compensation they would require to accept an increase in crime.

Revealed preference techniques infer valuations from the prices of related market-traded goods. One form of revealed preference builds up a value from the market values of constituent parts of the service or good being considered. This method could be used to value environmental amenities that affect the price of residential properties. For example, it can help us value clean air (and the cost of pollution) by estimating the premium placed on house prices in areas with clean air (or the discount on otherwise identical houses in polluted areas). Another example might be to look at wage differentials that people require to take on certain risks, to calculate how they value different aspects of their lives. This is called hedonic pricing.

Another approach recognises that people are generally willing to travel some distance to access goods and services on which they place a value. This inconvenience can be translated into money to derive the estimate of the benefits of those goods and services. This is called the **travel cost method.**

You can also look at **average household spending** on categories like 'leisure', 'health' or 'home improvement' to reveal how much people value these types of activity, relative to others. This type of data is often available from government surveys. In England, the Family Spending Survey can be a useful source.

When identifying proxies it is important to remember that we are not interested in whether money actually changes hands. It also doesn't matter whether or not the stakeholders in question could afford to buy something – they can still place a value on it. We assume that health has a similar value to people on any income. So, for example, you may want to use the average cost of health insurance as a proxy for improved health amongst children in care. The fact that those children would not be in a position to take out such insurance is beside the point – it gives generic guidance on how people value health.

There are problems with each of these techniques, and there are no hard and fast rules as to which you would use in given situations. We offer them to support you in deriving proxies. Nonetheless, this section requires creativity and research on your part, as well as consultation with your stakeholders to identify the most appropriate values. The following table gives examples of proxies that have been used in previous SROI analyses. For most outcomes we suggest a range of different possible proxies to help your own brainstorming.

Stakeholder	Outcome	Indicator	Possible Proxies
Person with mental health problem	Improvement in mental health	• Amount of time spent socialising • Extent to which participants engage in new activities • Level of use of mental health services	• Cost of membership of a social club/network • Percentage of income normally spent on leisure, • Cost of counselling sessions
Local community	Improved access to local services	• Take-up of those services, and by whom	• Savings in time and travel costs of being able to access services locally
Person with physical health problem	Improved physical health	• Number of visits to GP surgery • Extent of improvements in health (self-reported) • How often they exercise	• Cost of visiting private GP clinic • Cost of health insurance • Cost of gym membership
Care giver	Improved wellbeing	• Number of hours respite/ spent in leisure activities	• Value of hours spent engaged in these activities
The environment	Less waste	• Amount of waste going to landfill • Level of carbon emissions	• Cost of landfill charges • Cost of CO2 emissions
Prisoners' families	Improved relationships with family and social ties	• Number of family visits • Satisfaction with family visits	• Cost and time spent on travel
Young people	Decrease in drug use	• Level of drug use	• Average amount spent by young people on drugs
Offenders	Reduced reoffending	• Frequency of offences for which participant is charged • Nature of offence	• Forgone wages due to time spent in prison or doing community service
Care leaver	Reduced homeless-ness	• Access housing upon leaving care • Satisfaction with appropriateness of housing	• Rent • Cost of hostel accommodation
Woman offender	Improved family relationship	• Child continues living in the family home	• Amount that parents spend on their children annually • Value of time spent with children • Cost of childcare
Local community	Improved perception of the local area	• Residents report improvements in local area	• Change in property prices • Amount spent on home improvements

Identifying your financial proxies
Your stakeholders will be a good starting point for finding your proxies because only they know what it is they value and so know best how this might be captured.

While they may not be able to identify a tangible value, they can guide you as to what the change is worth to them.

As you check the proxy with stakeholders and see increasing agreement, the proxy may gain credibility. Where there is disagreement on values it is possible that the outcomes need to be expressed differently, otherwise it may be necessary to use average values. Often you can find academic articles or other research that has already assigned a monetary value to the outcome you are interested in. You'll still need to check that it is appropriate to your case.

Information on unit costs may be available from:

- websites maintained by the stakeholder who might gain from the cost saving (eg government departments like the Department for Work and Pensions);

- research into costs by government or independent bodies. The Personal Social Services Research Unit (www.pssru.ac.uk), for example, publishes comprehensive unit cost data for health and social care on an annual basis;

- your own estimates or research with the stakeholder on how much the saving would be.

Information on changes in income can be obtained from a range of places, including:

- data from stakeholders;

- reference to the average increase in a sample of your stakeholders;

- reference to other research of average increases that occur as a result of similar activities relating to the same outcomes.

Be careful with unit costs when calculating actual financial savings
Information on cost savings is often available in the form of unit costs. Unit costs are sometimes calculated as the total cost of an activity divided by the number of people benefiting from the activity. This includes both fixed costs, like the cost of a building, as well as variable costs, eg day-to-day running. The fixed costs may remain the same regardless of the number of participants in an activity. For example, the unit cost of housing a prisoner is in the region of £40,000 per annum when the total cost of the prison estate is divided by the number of prisoners. But if 100 people are prevented from going to prison that does not affect the fixed costs and is unlikely to achieve the full unit cost reduction per prisoner.

When you use unit costs be careful not to overstate the savings. The cost savings that you use should be the change in costs arising from your activity, called the **marginal costs**. Marginal costs will vary depending on the scale of the activity.

The problem is that data on marginal costs is harder to access, whereas unit costs are more routinely calculated.

Remember also that the department investing is not necessarily the one that makes the final saving. It is quite common for central government to benefit from cost savings that result from a local government initiative (eg prison savings from a reduction in crime) and vice versa. Even within an organisation it is possible that the cost saving would not be made by the department funding the activity but by another. Separating out stakeholders is necessary to avoid confusion and help communication.

Choosing credible financial proxies

It is important when communicating social value to understand that some proxies are more credible than others for different stakeholders. The most credible proxies have been used before (by third party sources with existing credibility), or are at least based on research undertaken by your organisation. Other proxies are market comparisons (what it would cost to achieve the same outcome) or working assumptions that will need to be related to proposed future improvements. These latter two may be necessary but are usually less credible.

When we get to sensitivity analysis you will have the opportunity to test the overall impact that the proxies have on your analysis. If you are having difficulties choosing between two proxies, make a note of them and later test what difference using either of them would make.

Top Tip: Proxies and double counting
It is possible to have the same financial proxy for different indicators without double counting. For example, if an activity improves the relationship between family members the same proxy (for example, the proportion of family income spent on children) may be applicable for both parents and children because it represents the value to each of them of the intervention. The total value is therefore the sum of these.

The worked example – financial proxies
Look at the Impact Map for Wheels-to-Meals on page 103: the blue section shows you how the column for financial proxies has been completed.
For example, for the outcome of 'fewer hospital admissions', desk research showed that this was not accounted for as a single figure. A hospital admission and stay was built up of a number of interventions from admission through to continuing care. Furthermore, costs varied for different patient groups, so the proxies chosen by Wheels-to-Meals were specific to older people. The source of these was the NHS cost book.

These proxies are examples of indirect cost savings. The change would not by itself result in a smaller budget or reduced spend for nearby hospitals in following years as there would be many more people in need of these services. Also, seven fewer admissions would not make a significant difference amongst all the other factors that affect the budgets. However, the costs identified are good proxies for this outcome and produce an appropriate way of valuing the change.

Other proxies were considered for the reduction in 'neighbourly care/shopping and breakdown of informal community networks' outcome. For example, Wheels-to-Meals considered whether the value of the neighbour's time might be a better financial proxy to use. They found a median wage using NOMIS (Annual Survey of Hours and Earnings – www.nomisweb.co.uk). If a neighbour were going shopping anyway, then the time involved would be the extra time they spent with residents before and/or after the shopping trip; they guessed this would total about half an hour. At the hourly median wage of £11.97 for half an hour per shopping trip this would be £5.99 per trip. As this was similar value to that used on the Impact Map for a supermarket online delivery fee, they felt more certain using the latter proxy.

Over to you: Financial proxies
You can now complete the sections on the Impact Map relating to financial proxies.

Stage 4:
Establishing Impact

This section provides a number of ways of assessing whether the outcomes you have analysed result from your activities. These methods provide a way of estimating how much of the outcome would have happened anyway and what proportion of the outcome can be isolated as being added by your activities. This is what we mean when we use the term impact.

Establishing impact is important as it reduces the risk of over-claiming and means that your story will be more credible. It is only by measuring and accounting for all of these factors that a sense of the impact that the activity is having can be gained. Otherwise there is the risk of investing in initiatives that don't work, or don't work as well as intended. As you will see, establishing impact may also help you identify any important stakeholders that you have missed.

There are four parts to this section:

4.1   Deadweight and displacement
4.2   Attribution
4.3   Drop-off
4.4   Calculating your impact

4.1 Deadweight and displacement

Deadweight is a measure of the amount of outcome that would have happened even if the activity had not taken place. It is calculated as a percentage. For example, an evaluation of a regeneration programme found that there has been a 7% increase in economic activity in the area since the programme began. However, the national economy grew by 5% during this time. Researchers would need to investigate how much of the local economic growth was due to wider economic changes and how much to the specific intervention being analysed.

To calculate deadweight, reference is made to comparison groups or benchmarks.[1] The perfect comparison would be the same group of people that you have affected, but seeing what happened to them if they had not benefited from the intervention.

Therefore, measuring deadweight will always be an estimate since a perfect comparison is not possible. Instead, you need to seek out information that is as close to your population as possible. The more similar the comparison group, the better the estimate will be.

Ask stakeholders about their services

In an evaluative SROI analysis, information on deadweight can be gathered during the data collection phase. For example, you may be able to ask stakeholders what other services they access and how helpful they find them. Or they may be able to tell you if they could have accessed another similar facility in the area anyway.

However, you will often have to go elsewhere for the kind of information you need. Data on some indicators will be available from government sources, both from individual departments and from organisations like the Office for National Statistics. Other information is sometimes available from infrastructure, member, trade or sector groups that represent the interests of particular stakeholders.

The simplest way to assess deadweight would be to look at the trend in the indicator over time to see if there is a difference between the trend before the activity started and the trend after the activity started. Any increase in the trend after the activity started provides an indication of how much of the outcome was the result of the activity.

There is a risk that the same change in the trend is happening elsewhere in a wider population of which your stakeholder group is a part. It is therefore better to also compare the trend in the indicator with trends in the wider population.

There is still a risk that whilst there is a change in the indicator relative to the wider population, the change happened to similar groups elsewhere, relative to their wider populations, where a similar intervention or activity was not available. The solution to this risk would be to calculate and compare the relative changes for both your stakeholder group and a similar group elsewhere.

1   Sometimes referred to as the counterfactual.

Here are some examples of data you could use to calculate deadweight for different kinds of outcome.

Outcome	Benchmark indicator
Reduction in reoffending rates among young ex-offenders (16-24 yrs) taking part in a rehabilitation programme	National average reoffending rate among 16-24-year-olds
Improvement in educational outcomes for young people in high-quality residential care homes	Educational outcomes for children in the residential care population as a whole
Increase in number of long-term unemployed gaining a job after participating in an employment training programme	Average rate at which the long-term unemployed come off benefits in the same region
Decreased crime in a borough after a borough-wide initiative increasing the number of police on the streets	Change in crime rate in a borough with similar socio-economic profile, but not subject to a specific crime-reduction initiative

Whether you want to understand your impact, or be more credible in your discussions with stakeholders, one advantage of calculating deadweight is that it weights the social value towards outcomes for stakeholders where deadweight is low. For what are sometimes called 'hard to reach' groups, deadweight is likely to be lower than for other groups. For example, the likelihood of someone who has been long-term homeless moving into employment without support is low; the likelihood is that much, if not all, of the change is due to the support received. This means that if the two groups experienced similar outcomes the impact would be higher for the harder to reach group.

As deadweight increases, your contribution to the outcome declines. When deadweight is high this may mean that the outcome is no longer material to your analysis.

Deadweight will be measured as a percentage and then that percentage of the outcome is deducted from the total quantity of the outcome.

Displacement is another component of impact and is an assessment of how much of the outcome displaced other outcomes. This does not apply in every SROI analysis but it is important to be aware of the possibility. Two examples show where displacement is most relevant:

1. An evaluation of a state-funded street lighting programme in one borough found a reduction in crime; however, the neighbouring borough reported an increase in crime during the same period. It is possible that the reduced crime was simply displaced.

2. A project supporting ex-offenders into employment counted the contribution to economic output, decreased benefit payments and increased taxes in its analysis. From the point of view of the state these benefits would have a high displacement rate as these are most likely jobs that are now denied to someone else that could have made similar contributions. This is irrespective of any other economic benefits to the individual or community that this project might produce.

If you think that displacement is relevant and your activities are displacing outcomes, you may find that there is now another stakeholder being affected by the displacement. You could go back and introduce the new stakeholder into the impact map or you could estimate the percentage of your outcomes that are double counted because there is some displacement, calculate the amount using this percentage and deduct it from the total.

Top Tip: Set yourself a limit on how much time you spend gathering data to establish impact
Do not spend too much time searching for information that you think should be available. You might consider setting a time limit on this stage. Always remember: the purpose of establishing impact is to help your organisation manage change. Avoid spending too long chasing false accuracy. This means you should be comfortable with estimates that are based on the best available information.

The worked example – deadweight and displacement
Look at the Impact Map for Wheels-to-Meals on page 104: the yellow section shows you how the column for deadweight has been completed.

For example, for the outcome of 'healthier volunteers', although the luncheon club had a demonstrable effect on the amount of physical activity reported by all volunteers, it was considered that if they hadn't been volunteering for Wheels-to-Meals they might have been volunteering somewhere else or doing other things with this time (such as going for a walk) that would have led to the same outcome. However, as part of the volunteer annual assessment the volunteers identified that the luncheon club involved more physical exercise than they might have otherwise sought. Volunteers were asked to estimate how much more. The average was around 45% more. So if the benchmark is 100%, because all of them would have done some other exercise anyway, the increase is therefore 145%. The estimate of deadweight is 100%/145% or 70%. This was used as the estimate for the activity that would have happened anyway.

For the outcome of 'residents having nutritious meals', the nutritious meals, and resulting health improvements, were identified as the change that the council expected. However, this change would have happened anyway: if Wheels-to-Meals were not delivering this contract, the council would have another provider deliver it, as a meals-on-wheels service, to a similar standard of nutrition (specified in the contract). So deadweight is 100%. This will result in no impact on our impact map for this row. However, we will still show the row as it is a part of the story of change.

In this example, displacement has not been considered.

Over to you: Deadweight and displacement

You can now complete the section on the Impact Map relating to deadweight and displacement. Although there is no space to record the rationale and the sources, you need to keep a record of these so that they can be included in your report.

4.2 Attribution

Attribution is an assessment of how much of the outcome was caused by the contribution of other organisations or people. Attribution is calculated as a percentage (ie the proportion of the outcome that is attributable to your organisation). It shows the part of deadweight for which you have better information and where you can attribute outcome to other people or organisations.

For example, alongside a new cycling initiative there is a decrease in carbon emissions in a borough. However, at the same time, a congestion charge and an environmental awareness programme began. While the cycling initiative knows that it has contributed because of the number of motorists that have switched to cycling, it will need to determine what share of the reduced emissions it can claim and how much is down to the other initiatives.

It will never be possible to get a completely accurate assessment of attribution. This stage is more about being aware that your activity may not be the only one contributing to the change observed than getting an exact calculation. It is about checking that you have included all the relevant stakeholders.

Reassess your stakeholders

The first question is whether there are any organisations or people that contribute to the outcomes that you haven't included – these are missing stakeholders.

It is also possible that the contributions made by organisations and people in the past should be taken into account. For example, a person seeking work may gain that job because of your support in training as well as another organisation's support with preparing CVs and helping with interview techniques.

Where different stakeholders had other support in the past it may be useful to consider them as different groups of stakeholders. For example, children in care may have different journeys through the system depending on their experiences prior to coming into care.

As a result you may want to reconsider your stakeholders and split them into groups that had different experiences before their involvement with your activity. If you don't go back and include the new stakeholder and the inputs that they make then you will need to estimate the attribution. Either you will increase the overall inputs included in the Impact Map or you will have to reduce the outcome attributed to the existing inputs.

There are three main approaches to estimating attribution. You may want to use a combination of these methods to make your estimate as robust as possible:

1. Base your estimate on your experience. For example, you have been working with other organisations for a number of years and have a good idea of how you each contribute to the outcomes.

2. **Ask stakeholders** – both existing ones and any new ones you have identified – what percentage of the outcome is the result of your activity. In an evaluative SROI analysis this could be conducted during the data collection phase, through surveys, focus groups or interview.

3. Consult with the other organisations to which you think there is attribution. You could find out how much they all spend towards meeting the objective and attribute according to the amount they spend on a unit of outcome. Of course, this assumes that all expenditure is equally effective. Alternatively, you could have conversations with these organisations (even a joint meeting) to understand how they all contribute to the client's journey and then work out percentages that they can claim credit for on that basis.

Common mistakes with attribution
There are three common mistakes that people make with attribution:

1. Remember that the purpose of the estimate of attribution is to help your organisation manage change – but it will be an estimate. So don't spend too long on this, but do explain how you have reached your estimate.

2. Take care not to attribute outcomes to organisations or people that are being paid out of the inputs (investment) that you recorded in Stage 2, as the investment takes account of their contribution.

3. As attribution may have been included as part of your estimate of deadweight, take care not to take off more than you should from your outcomes. This will depend on the quality of the benchmark used.

The worked example – attribution
Look at the Impact Map for Wheels-to-Meals on page 104; the yellow section shows you how the column for attribution has been completed.

For example: for the attribution of 'more socialising' outcome, Wheels-to-Meals used a questionnaire to ask residents if they had joined clubs and groups as a result of the luncheon club. Because it is difficult to justify that this is entirely down to Wheels-to-Meals the questionnaire also asked if other friends and organisations had recommended or promoted clubs and groups, and, if so, how important this had been to the decision to join. Based on the results in the questionnaire it was possible to estimate that 35% of the outcome was the result of the contributions of others.

Over to you: Attribution

You can now complete the section on the Impact Map relating to attribution by putting in a percentage. Although there is no space to record the rationale for your attribution and its source you need to keep a record of this somewhere so that it can be included in your report.

You should record a description of any organisations or people relating to attribution and a description of the relationship to your work. This will form part of your report.

4.3 Drop-off

In Stage 3.3 we considered how long the outcomes lasted. In future years, the amount of outcome is likely to be less or, if the same, will be more likely to be influenced by other factors, so attribution to your organisation is lower. Drop-off is used to account for this and is only calculated for outcomes that last more than one year.

For example, an initiative to improve the energy efficiency of social housing has great short-term success in reducing energy bills and carbon emissions. However, as time passes, the systems wear out and get replaced with cheaper but less efficient systems. Unless you have built up some historical data on the extent to which the outcome reduces over time, you will need to estimate the amount of drop-off, and we recommend a standard approach in the absence of other information. You can inform this estimate with research, such as academic sources, or by talking to people who have been involved in similar activities in the past.

Drop-off is usually calculated by deducting a fixed percentage from the remaining level of outcome at the end of each year. For example, an outcome of 100 that lasts for three years but drops off by 10% per annum would be 100 in the first year, 90 in the second (100 less 10%) and 81 in the third (90 less 10%).

Over the longer term you will need to have a management system that allows you to measure this ongoing value more accurately. However, it is likely that you will need to track your participants as part of your data collection anyway, so questions to evidence drop-off can be included.

Over to you: Drop-off

You can now complete the section on the Impact Map relating to drop-off by putting in a percentage. Although there is no space to record the rationale for your drop-off and its source, you need to keep a record of this so that it can be included in your report. You won't make use of this until Stage 5, Calculating your SROI.

Stage 4

4.4 Calculating your impact

All of these aspects of impact are normally expressed as percentages. Unless you have more accurate information it is acceptable to round estimates to the nearest 10%. In some cases you might consider that there is an increase in the value rather than a reduction. However, we do not recommend that you increase your impact as a result of considering these issues. In this situation you would simply not make a deduction. Your Impact Map should now have percentages filled in for deadweight, attribution, drop-off and (if applicable) displacement. You can calculate your impact for each outcome as follows:

- Financial proxy multiplied by the quantity of the outcome gives you a total value. From this total you deduct any percentages for deadweight or attribution.

- Repeat this for each outcome (to arrive at the impact for each)

- Add up the total (to arrive at the overall impact of the outcomes you have included)

The worked example – calculating impact
This is how Wheels-to-Meals staff calculated the impact for one of the indicators, 'clubs and groups joined'.

First, they took the quantity of each outcome and multiplied by the financial proxy. This gives the total value of the outcome.

| Total outcomes | 16 x £48.25 | = £772.00 |

Then they deducted the deadweight, or what would have happened anyway.

Less deadweight	£772 - 10% (or 90% of £772)	
	90% of £772	
	0.9 x £772	= £694.80

Next they accounted for attribution, or how much of the change was down to others.

| Less attribution | £694.80 - 35% | |
| | £694.80 x 0.65 | = £451.62 |

For that row, this is the value of the impact created during the period of the scope – the year of the luncheon club being analysed.

Look at the Impact Map for Wheels-to-Meals on page 104; the yellow section shows you how these columns have been completed.

Over to you: Impact
You can now complete the section on the Impact Map relating to impact.

Stage 4

Stage 5:
Calculating the SROI

You will now have collected all the information together to enable you to calculate your SROI. You will also have recorded qualitative and quantitative information that you will need in the report. As you will want people to read your report, remember to keep the information you include to a minimum. This stage sets out how to summarise the financial information that you have recorded in the previous stages. The basic idea is to calculate the financial value of the investment and the financial value of the social costs and benefits. This results in two numbers – and there are several different ways of reporting on the relationship between these numbers.

If you are carrying out an evaluative SROI analysis, then the evaluation should ideally take place after the period for which the outcome was expected to last. However, interim evaluations will still be useful in order to assess how well the intervention is working and to provide information to support any changes. If you are comparing actual results against a forecast you will need the information relating to the time periods over which your outcomes last.

There are four steps to calculating your ratio, with an optional fifth:

5.1   Projecting into the future
5.2   Calculating the net present value
5.3   Calculating the ratio
5.4   Sensitivity analysis
5.5   Payback period

All these stages will be outlined below. We will discuss each step before asking you to do your own calculations.

5.1 Projecting into the future

The first step in calculating your ratio is to project the value of all the outcomes achieved into the future. In step 3.3, above, you decided how long an outcome would last. Using this, you will now need to:

- set out the value of the impact (from step 4.4) for each outcome for one time period (usually 1 year);

- copy the value for each outcome across the number of time periods it will last (as recorded in the Duration column on your impact map); then

- subtract any drop-off you identified (step 4.3) for each of the future time periods after the first year.

In the worked example this was done using Excel. We have not included an example of a blank Excel sheet because different people have different approaches to Excel and because we have found that standard approaches cannot be easily used for different situations. It is easier to set up your own spreadsheet using the worked example and the description in the text as a guide.[1]

The worked example – drop-off and impact projected in future years
Look at the impact map for Wheels-to-Meals on page 104: the yellow section shows you how the columns for impact have been completed.

If we take the line for GP practice nurse group sessions, the duration is 5 years and the drop-off 10%. The 10% is an estimation of the likelihood that residents will use the knowledge they gain less as time goes on as they forget the sessions.

So the calculation Wheels-to-Meals used to work out the effect of drop-off on the projected impact into future years goes like this:

Impact in year 1   = £1,539.00

This is the same as the impact calculated at the end of the project. We only account for the outcomes in the year after the activity and only calculate drop-off in following years.

Impact in year 2	yr1 impact less drop-off	
	£1,539.00 less 10%	
	£1,539.00 x 0.9	= £1,385.10
Impact in year 3	yr2 impact less drop-off	
	£1,385.10 less 10%	
	£1,385.10 x 0.9	= £1,246.59
Impact in year 4	yr3 impact less drop-off	
	£1,246.59 less 10%	
	£1,246.59 x 0.9	= £1,121.93

---

1   See www.thesroinetwork.org for information on developments in software that will assist in completing this stage.

Impact in year 5

yr4 impact less drop-off
£1,121.93 less 10%
£1,121.93 x 0.9 = £1,009.74

5.2 Calculating the net present value

In order to calculate the net present value (NPV) the costs and benefits paid or received in different time periods need to be added up. In order that these costs and benefits are comparable a process called discounting is used. Discounting recognises that people generally prefer to receive money today rather than tomorrow because there is a risk (eg, that the money will not be paid) or because there is an opportunity cost (eg, potential gains from investing the money elsewhere). This is known as the 'time value of money'. An individual may have a high discount rate – for example, if you would accept £2 in one year's time, instead of £1 now, that implies a discount rate of 100%.

This is a controversial area and one where there is ongoing research and discussion. The main problem with using discounting in SROI is that it encourages short-termism by discounting the future. This is especially problematic for environmental outcomes, where the value may even increase. This betrays the extent to which people actually value their future and their children's future.

There is a range of different rates. For the public sector, the basic rate recommended in HM Treasury's *Green Book* is 3.5%. The Stern Review on the economics of climate change argued that it was not ethically defensible for pure time preference to be applied to cost-benefit calculations where these involved significant wealth transfers from the future to the present and used lower rates. Following the Stern Review, HM Treasury published supplementary guidance on intergenerational wealth transfers, in which a reduced discount rate of 3%, which eliminates the pure time preference element, is applied alongside the usual discount rate.[2]

This issue is under review by the Measuring Social Value consortium, and the aim is to produce further guidance on discounting in due course.

The process is to discount the projected values over time, as you set out in stage 5.1, above. This can be easily done if you are using Excel, which has functions for calculating Present Value and Net Present Value.

Although this calculation is automated in Excel (=NPV, discount rate, value1, value 2…), it may be useful to know how the calculation for Present Value works and this is shown below ('r' represents the discount rate):

2   More information on the different elements that make up the discount rate is set out in Annex 6 of the *Green Book*.

Stage 5

| Present Value | = | Value of impact in Year 1 $(1+r)$ | + | Value of impact in Year 2 $(1+r)^2$ | + | Value of impact in Year 3 $(1+r)^3$ | + | Value of impact in Year 4 $(1+r)^4$ | + | Value of impact in Year 5 $(1+r)^5$ |

Here is a fictional example for an organisation called Youth Work, where r = 3.5%, or 0.035.

	Year 1	Year 2	Year 3	Year 4	Year 5
Benefits	£448,875	£414,060	£389,935	£355,648	£319,005
Discounted Values =	$\dfrac{£448,875}{(1.035)}$ +	$\dfrac{£414,060}{(1.035)^2}$ +	$\dfrac{£389,935}{(1.035)^3}$ +	$\dfrac{£355,648}{(1.035)^4}$ +	$\dfrac{£319,005}{(1.035)^5}$
Present Value =	1,750,444				

Having calculated the Present Value of your benefits, you can deduct the value of your inputs (the investment) to arrive at the Net Present Value (NPV).

NPV   =   [Present value of benefits] - [Value of investments]

In the Youth Work example the investment was £576,000. Therefore, the net present value would be calculated as follows:

NPV   =   £1,750,444 - £576,000
      =   £1,174,444

5.3 Calculating the ratio

You are now in a position to calculate the initial SROI ratio. This is a very simple sum. You divide the discounted value of benefits by the total investment.

SROI ratio   = $\dfrac{\text{Present Value}}{\text{Value of inputs}}$

An alternative calculation is the net SROI ratio. This divides the NPV by the value of the investment. Both are acceptable but you need to be clear which you have used.

Net SROI ratio   = $\dfrac{\text{Net Present Value}}{\text{Value of inputs}}$

**The worked example – calculating the SROI
(discounting and net present value)**

Look at the Impact Map for Wheels-to-Meals on page 105: the green section shows you the value of the discounted benefits.

Using Excel and the NPV function, the total present value of our example has been calculated following the above method. Wheels-to-Meals also used the 3.5% discount rate.

Total present value	= £81,741.93

Net present value	total present value - total inputs	
	£81,741.93 - £42,375	= £39,366.93

SROI	total present value / total inputs	
	£81,741.93 / £42,375	= £1.93: £1

So for Wheels-to-Meals, there is £1.93 of value for every £1 of investment.

5.4 Sensitivity analysis

One of the strengths of setting up a spreadsheet is that it is possible to assess the importance of elements of the model relatively easily; by altering the figures, the spreadsheet will make all the changes to the calculation for you. After calculating the ratio, it is important to assess the extent to which your results would change if you changed some of the assumptions you made in the previous stages. The aim of such an analysis is to test which assumptions have the greatest effect on your model.

The standard requirement is to check changes to:

* estimates of deadweight, attribution and drop-off;

* financial proxies;

* the quantity of the outcome; and

* the value of inputs, where you have valued non-financial inputs.

The recommended approach is to calculate how much you need to change each estimate in order to make the social return become a social return ratio of £1 value for £1 investment. By calculating this, the sensitivity of your analysis to changes in estimates can be shown. This allows you to report the amount of change necessary to make the ratio change from positive to negative or vice versa.

 We are interested in which changes have a significant impact on the overall ratio. It is these that you would consider as potential priority areas in managing the value you are creating. For example, if your result is sensitive to changes in a particular indicator you may want to prioritise investment in systems to manage (and resources to improve performance in) that indicator.

In general the greater the change that you need to make in order for the SROI to become £1 for every £1 invested, the more likely it is that the result is not sensitive. It is also possible that a choice you made earlier between two proxies is now resolved because the choice doesn't affect the overall ratio. All of these findings should be discussed in the final SROI report.

This focus on the significant issues will help you keep your report short.

The worked example – sensitivity analysis

Let us consider, as an example, how Wheels-to-Meals explored the sensitivity of the top row of the Impact Map, which covers the outcome 'fewer falls' (you will need to consider all rows). This was a useful row to work with as it resulted in the biggest financial value on the Impact Map, so needed scrutiny.

- Impact. Low deadweight and attribution were identified in this row. This could be an issue. What if this was wrong and, for example, more of this change was down to others than Wheels-to-Meals had realised? How far out would the attribution figure have to be for the SROI to fall to £1: £1?

  Using the spreadsheet to change the numbers and repeat the calculations, attribution would have needed to be 53% for the SROI to become £1: £1 rather than the 5% we have identified. If this were the case, the impact would fall from a total for this row of £81,648 (for all three financial proxies) to £40,394, reducing the SROI to £1: £1.

  The change in attribution from 5% to 53% is a 960% increase.

- Financial proxies. There are three financial proxies in this row. As an example, we will see how Wheels-to-Meals assessed the sensitivity of the financial proxy from the NHS cost book for 'geriatric continuing care inpatient'.

  The change required to this figure (in this case a reduction) for the SROI to fall to £1:£1 is for the financial proxy to drop from £7,220 per admission/stay to £1,093 – a change of 85%. This figure is, therefore, more sensitive, although the value would still need to change significantly, so Wheels-to-Meals felt that the proxies it had chosen were adequate.

Remember that the SROI figure is based on an incomplete example and this has implications for the sensitivity analysis. The point of the example is to show how it is applied.

It would also be possible to now present the results from a different perspective. For example, if the cost of admission/stay fell to just over £1,093, the social return of Wheels-to-Meals would still be more than £1: £1.

5.5 Payback period (optional)

The 'payback period' describes how long it would take for an investment to be paid off. Specifically, it answers the question: at what point in time does the value of the social returns start to exceed the investment? Many funders and investors use this kind of calculation as a way of determining risk in a project. While a short payback period may be less risky, a long payback period is often a feature of activities that can generate significant long-term outcomes, thus longer-term core funding is required.

Often the investment will be paid back over a period of months rather than whole years and so is reported in months. Assuming that the annual impact is the same each year, the first step is to divide the annual impact for all participants by 12 to get impact per month. Then divide the investment by the impact per month to get payback period in months.

The basic formula is:

$$\text{Payback Period in Months} = \frac{\text{Investment}}{\text{Annual impact}/12}$$

Over to you: Financial projections

You can now complete your financial projections on your Impact Map.

Stage 6:
Reporting, using and embedding

Congratulations! You now have a completed SROI analysis.

However, the process is not complete. There is a final important stage: reporting to your stakeholders, communicating and using the results, and embedding the SROI process in your organisation. This stage gives guidance on how to make the most of all of your hard work so far.

The three issues to consider are:

6.1 Reporting to stakeholders
6.2 Using the results
6.3 Assurance

6.1 Reporting to stakeholders

You need to make sure that the way in which you communicate the results is relevant to the audiences that you decided upon when you set your scope. Your findings may be for internal management use, for public distribution or as the basis for different discussions with different stakeholders. Preparing a report is useful because it is the place where you can make recommendations to influence what happens as your organisation or project moves forward.

SROI aims to create accountability to stakeholders. As such it is important that the results are communicated to stakeholders in a meaningful way. This involves more than publishing the results on your website. You may well find that external stakeholders are very interested to hear about your work with SROI – both the process you went through and the results.

Your final report should comprise much more than the social returns calculated. The SROI report should include qualitative, quantitative and financial aspects to provide the user with the important information on the social value being created in the course of an activity. It tells the story of change and explains the decisions you made in the course of your analysis.

The report should include enough information to allow another person to be assured that your calculations are robust and accurate. That is, it needs to include all the decisions and assumptions you made along the way. To help your organisation improve it should include all the information that you were able to find out about the performance of the organisation which might be useful to strategic planning and the way it conducts its activities. You will need to be aware of commercial sensitivities in deciding what you include in the report.

An SROI report should be as short as possible while meeting principles of transparency and materiality. It should also be consistent, using a structured framework that allows comparison between reports. Details of the contents of an SROI report can be found in the Resources section. However, the following quantitative and qualitative information is usually included in a comprehensive and considered SROI report:

- information relating to your organisation, including a discussion of its work, key stakeholders and activities;

- description of the scope of the analysis, details of stakeholder involvement, methods of data collection, and any assumptions and limitations underlying the analysis;

- the impact map, with relevant indicators and any proxies;

- case studies, or quotes from participants that illustrate particular findings;

- details of the calculations, and a discussion of any estimates and assumptions. This section would include the sensitivity analysis and a description of the effect of varying your assumptions on social returns;

- an audit trail for decision-making, including which stakeholders, outcomes or indicators were included and which were not, and a rationale for each of these decisions;

- an executive summary aimed at a broad audience, including participants.

Try and present your findings in a balanced way; how you phrase your recommendations may affect how they are taken up. It is important, therefore, to stress the positive as well as negative findings and to present them in a sensitive fashion.

It is also important to be able to distinguish between benefits that are not happening and benefits that may be happening but cannot be evidenced. Make sure to include recommendations for ways to improve data collection and evidencing outcomes.

Top Tip: Presentation of social return calculations
There is a risk, and perhaps a temptation, to focus on the social return ratio. However, the number by itself does not have much meaning – it is merely a shorthand way of expressing all of the value that you have calculated so far. In the same way, financial investors need more than the ratio – it would be an unwise investor who based their investment decisions purely on one number. Therefore, the ratio should be presented alongside the other information, such as the story of how change is being created and case studies from participants.

Example: Executive summary for MillRace IT
This is an extract from the executive summary of MillRace IT's SROI report. It is an example of how to combine the rest of the story about social value creation with the numbers generated by the calculations.

'The aggregate social value created by MillRace IT each year is projected to be approximately £76,825. MillRace IT's SROI ratio of 7.4:1 implies that, for every £1 invested, £7.40 of social value is created each year for society in terms of reduced healthcare costs, reduced benefits costs, and increased taxes collected.'

As the SROI analysis demonstrates, MillRace IT creates value in two key ways. First, by participating in MillRace IT, clients get long-term support and avoid a relapse in their condition. Second, a number of participants leave MillRace IT to go on to employment. By creating a supportive environment and teaching marketable skills in an area where there is much demand, MillRace IT effectively combines financial sustainability and high-quality support for those recovering from mental ill health.

Over to you: Preparing the SROI report
Prepare your SROI report. Include findings, analysis, and recommendations as to what the organisation can learn from the information generated through the entire SROI process.

6.2 Using the results

Unless you do something as a result of carrying out your SROI analysis there was not much point in undertaking it in the first place. This is one of the most important parts of the SROI analysis but, often, one to which the least time and resources are dedicated. It is easy to overlook it after the 'excitement' of reaching the SROI ratio.

To be useful, the SROI analysis needs to result in change. Such change might be in how those that invest in your activities understand and support your work, or how those that commission your services describe, specify and manage the contract with you. However, there will also be implications for your organisation, whether you carried out an evaluative or forecast SROI analysis.

Changes following a forecast SROI analysis

The results of a forecast SROI analysis may make you review your planned activities in order to try and maximise the social value you plan to create. Its findings may also require you to review your planned systems for gathering information on outcome, deadweight, attribution and displacement. See if they need to be adapted for your next SROI analysis and change them accordingly. Following a forecast SROI analysis you may also want to build in ways to:

- systematically talk to your stakeholders about their intended outcomes and what they value; and

- work with partners to explore attribution.

Changes following an evaluative SROI analysis

An evaluative SROI analysis should result in changes in your organisation. Your organisation will need to respond to findings and think through implications for organisational objectives, governance, systems and working practices. Ensure that the organisation acts on the recommendations and that findings feed into your strategic planning process.

Your ratios will be very useful in communicating with stakeholders. However, where the ratio has most value is in how it changes over time. This can tell you comprehensively whether your activities are improving or not. This should also give your organisation information about how to change its services to maximise social value in future.

It is important to secure commitment to further SROI analyses. The way you approach this will vary depending on your role in the organisation. A starting point might be to present the findings from the study to staff, trustees and stakeholders, stressing the benefits as well as the challenges of the process. This would give you the opportunity to also present a plan for making SROI analysis a routine and regular component of the organisation's reporting. Such a plan should set out:

- a process for regular data collection, particularly for outcomes;

- a process for training staff to ensure knowledge and expertise is retained in your organisation even if there is turnover;

- a clear timeline for the next SROI analysis;

- a description of the resources that will be required for ongoing monitoring of SROI; and

- how data security will be ensured.

Change can be difficult, especially if you are a large organisation with complex management systems. Remember that the extent to which recommendations are taken up by your organisation will depend on the level of organisational buy-in you have achieved. This is why we have stressed involving stakeholders throughout the process. It is helpful to allocate responsibility for future SROI analyses. It may be that once the data collection mechanisms are in place the responsibility for assessing SROI can sit with your finance team and become integrated with the financial accounting system. Remember that these changes do not have to be put in place overnight, so set yourself a realistic timescale.

Top Tip: External stakeholders' comparison of SROI reports
The way in which external stakeholders and the wider public use published SROI reports will vary. Comparison of social return ratios is unlikely to be helpful, whereas an analysis of the different judgements and decisions made in completing an individual SROI report, and the proposed changes that those responsible for the activity are planning to make, will be much more useful. Similarly, comparing the changes in an organisation's ratios over time will guide investors as to the scale of improvements organisations are making. This highlights how important it is that the information is presented in ways that meet the requirements of different stakeholders and that there is independent assurance of the information.

See www.thesroinetwork.org for guidance for social investors and commissioners.

Over to you: Communicating and using findings, and embedding SROI
In presenting the results of your analysis, consider your audience, tailoring the discussion to each group of stakeholders. Stakeholders will have different objectives, and the relationship of each stakeholder to your organisation will vary.

Prepare a plan for using the findings and embedding the process within your organisation.

6.3 Assurance

Assurance is the process by which the information in your report is verified. The principle requires that there should be appropriate independent assurance of your report's claims. There are two levels of assurance:

Type 1 Assurance focuses on assurance that the analysis has complied with the principles of good practice in SROI.

Type 2 Assurance covers assurance of both principles and data.

For more information on the assurance processes and sources of support, refer to www.thesroinetwork.org.

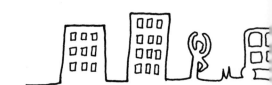

Resources

This section contains a number of resources that can be used as you go along.

1   Format for an SROI report
2   Glossary
3   Note on cost allocation
4   Note on capital or loan-financed projects
5   Sources of support and further information
6   Downloads
7   A summary of the relationship between SROI and other approaches
8   The seven principles of SROI
9   Checklist for SROI analysis
10   The worked example
11   A blank Impact Map (provided as a loose insert in the printed version of this guide, and also available as a download)

1 Format for an SROI report

The following sets out the key elements of an SROI report. Within the structure of the six stages there is flexibility about how the information can be presented. The information will be a balance between qualitative, quantitative and financial data that together describe the value resulting from the activities set out in the scope. The aim will be to provide enough information to comply with the principles and to provide evidence that the process has been followed.

Executive summary

1 Scope and stakeholders

A description of your organisation: its activities and values, the activity under analysis, including location, main customers or beneficiaries.

An explanation of SROI, the type undertaken and the purpose of the analysis. The time period of the activity.

One or two stakeholder case studies from the point of view of each stakeholder and a description of their journey of change.

A description of the theory of change: of how the activity is expected to achieve its objectives. A summary of organisations involved in attribution.

The analysis of the stakeholders and stakeholder groups.

The numbers of people or organisations in each stakeholder group.

Description of how stakeholders were involved.

The numbers of people or organisations from each group that were involved in developing the theory of change for that stakeholder group.

2 Outcomes and evidence

Description of inputs, outputs and outcomes for each stakeholder group. Outcomes will include changes that are positive, negative, intended and unintended.

Description of the indicators and data sources used for each outcome.

Quantity of inputs, outputs and outcomes achieved for each stakeholder group.

Analysis of the investment required for the activity.

The length of time over which the outcome is expected to last, or against which the outcome will be attributed to the activity.

Description of the financial proxy to be used for each outcome, together with the source of the information for each proxy.

3 Impact

Description of the other areas or groups against which deadweight is estimated.

Description of the other organisations or people to which outcomes have been attributed.

The basis for any estimates of attribution and deadweight.

% attribution for each indicator of outcome with a financial proxy.

% deadweight for each indicator of outcome with a financial proxy.

% drop-off for each indicator of outcome with a financial proxy.

Description of displacement, if included.

The total impact.

4 Social return calculation

Calculation of the social return, showing sources of information, including a description of the type or types of social return calculation used.

A description of the sensitivity analysis carried out and why.

A description of the changes to quantities as a result of the sensitivity analysis.

A comparison of the social return in the sensitivity analysis.

5 Audit trail

Stakeholders identified but not included, and rationale for this.

Outcomes identified but not included, for each stakeholder, and the rationale.

Any financial proxies not included, and the rationale.

2 Glossary

Attribution   An assessment of how much of the outcome was caused by the contribution of other organisations or people.

Cost allocation   The allocation of costs or expenditure to activities related to a given programme, product or business.

Deadweight   A measure of the amount of outcome that would have happened even if the activity had not taken place.

Discounting   The process by which future financial costs and benefits are recalculated to present-day values.

Discount rate   The interest rate used to discount future costs and benefits to a present value.

Displacement   An assessment of how much of the outcome has displaced other outcomes.

Distance travelled   The progress that a beneficiary makes towards an outcome (also called 'intermediate outcomes').

Drop-off   The deterioration of an outcome over time.

Duration   How long (usually in years) an outcome lasts after the intervention, such as length of time a participant remains in a new job.

Financial value   The financial surplus generated by an organisation in the course of its activities.

Financial model   A set of relationships between financial variables that allow the effect of changes to variables to be tested.

Impact   The difference between the outcome for participants, taking into account what would have happened anyway, the contribution of others and the length of time the outcomes last.

Impact Map   A table that captures how an activity makes a difference: that is, how it uses its resources to provide activities that then lead to particular outcomes for different stakeholders.

Income   An organisation's financial income from sales, donations, contracts or grants.

Inputs	The contributions made by each stakeholder that are necessary for the activity to happen.
Materiality	Information is material if its omission has the potential to affect the readers' or stakeholders' decisions.
Monetise	To assign a financial value to something.
Net present value	The value in today's currency of money that is expected in the future minus the investment required to generate the activity.
Net social return ratio	Net present value of the impact divided by total investment.
Outcome	The changes resulting from an activity. The main types of change from the perspective of stakeholders are unintended (unexpected) and intended (expected), positive and negative change.
Outputs	A way of describing the activity in relation to each stakeholder's inputs in quantitative terms.
Outcome indicator	Well-defined measure of an outcome.
Payback period	Time in months or years for the value of the impact to exceed the investment.
Proxy	An approximation of value where an exact measure is impossible to obtain.
Scope	The activities, timescale, boundaries and type of SROI analysis.
Sensitivity analysis	Process by which the sensitivity of an SROI model to changes in different variables is assessed.
Social return ratio	Total present value of the impact divided by total investment.
Stakeholders	People, organisations or entities that experience change, whether positive or negative, as a result of the activity that is being analysed.

3 Note on cost allocation

The value of the contribution made by whoever is financing the activity will often be relatively easy to calculate – for example, where the activity is funded completely by one or more sources then the value of the contribution is known.

If the analysis relates to part of an organisation then it may be more difficult to calculate the investment being made. It is important to get this right so that the cost of producing social value is not understated. This is similar to full cost recovery in grant applications. Unless you identify the full cost of your activities (not just the grant funding, for example), you will not get an accurate ratio.

For example: in an organisation with two departments, where the analysis only relates to one department, it will be necessary to start by calculating how much the department costs. Most of the costs will be known and could be obtained from the accounts. The problem arises if the organisation buys things that are used by both departments (such as electricity or the organisation's manager). It will be necessary to allocate these costs to the department and then identify who provided the inputs (the investment that covered the costs). This may need some proportioning between sources of finance. It may be helpful to involve your accountant, if you have one, at this point.

Even when you are analysing the social return arising from, say, a grant, you will need to take care that the activity does not depend on other contributions from elsewhere in the organisation that are not being funded through the grant.

The steps are:

A. Identify costs for goods and services that are required for the activity you are analysing.

B. Identify and allocate the costs of goods and services that are shared by different departments.

C. Identify the sources of income for these goods and services.

D. If necessary, identify proportions of income from different sources.

A. Identify costs for goods and services that are required for the activity you are analysing

This can normally be done by reference to the organisation's accounts. If expenditure is not divided between different departments you will need to go through each type of expenditure and identify which costs wholly relate to the department you are analysing.

B. Identify and allocate the costs of goods and services that are shared by different departments

For those costs that are shared, you will need to decide how to allocate them. There are three main methods.

For **salary costs**, the costs can be allocated according to how much time the member of staff spends working for each department. If there are timesheets, these will provide the information. If there are not, then you will need to estimate. Some staff, such as the chief executive, may work across all the departments. In this case you can allocate their costs according to the relative size of the budget for each department.

For **non-salary costs**, it may be appropriate to allocate costs based on a measure of activity within the department – such as allocating electricity costs according to the overall expenditure on goods and services.

For **rent**, however, it would be more appropriate to allocate using the share of the overall floor space.

Resources

Example 1:

Costs in £000	Total costs	Department 1	Department 2
Manager (see point 1 below)	45	26	19
Training manager (see point 2 below)	40	24	16
Department staff, 1 in each department	30	15	15
Department non-staff costs, 20 for Department 1and 10 for Department 2	30	20	10
Subtotal for departments	60	35	25
Heat and light (see point 3 below)	20	13	7
Rent (see point 4 on next page)	20	5	15
Total	185	103	82

Figures have been rounded to the nearest whole number.

1 The manager's costs of £45,000 can be allocated according to the relative project costs. Overall, the project costs are £30,000 for staff and £30,000 for non-staff, a total of £60,000. However, this is not split evenly between the two departments. For Department 1 the costs are £35,000 (£15,000 for staff plus £20,000 for non-staff) and £25,000 (£15,000 for staff and £10,000 for non-staff) for Department 2.

   £35,000 divided by £60,000 multiplied by £45,000 equals £26,250 for Department 1. £25,000 divided by £60,000 multiplied by £45,000 equals £18,750 for Department 2. Rounded up or down, these are the relative costs of the manager's time spent on each project.

2 The training manager, who costs £40,000, spends 60% of their time in Department 1 and 40% in Department 2. 60% times £40,000 is 24,000.

3 The organisation cannot measure electricity usage by department and so has allocated costs based on department non-staff costs. £20,000 divided by £30,000 multiplied by £20,000 equals £13,333.

4 For rent, 20% of the available space is used by Department 1 and 70% by Department 2 The remaining 10% is used by the manager. 20% of £20,000 is £4,000. 70% of £20,000 is £14,000.

This still leaves £2,000 unallocated (£20,000 minus £14,000 minus £4,000) that relates to the manager. If this were allocated according to the share used by the manager (the departmental subtotal of £35,000 divided by £60,000), it would be split £1,200 and £800. So the total rent for Department 1 is £4,000 plus £1,200 equals £5,200 (rounded to £5,000). The rent for Department 2 is £14,000 plus £800 equals £14,800 (rounded to £15,000).

C. Identify the sources of income for these goods and services

These costs must now be allocated a second time, to those financing the activity. In Example 2, below, one of the sources has stated that all the finance must be used for Department 1 costs and has accepted the method for allocating these, as used above. The other source of income covers the balance in Department 1 and all of Department 2.

Example 2

Income	£000	Department 1	Department 2
Funder 1	100	100	
Funder 2	85	3	82
Total	185	103	82

D. If necessary, identify proportions of income from different sources

In contrast to Example 2, in Example 3, below, the sources can be used for the whole organisation's expenditure. £100,000 divided by £185,000 multiplied by £103,000 equals £56,000.

Example 3

Income	£000	Department 1	Department 2
Source 1	100	56	44
Source 2	85	47	38
Total	185	103	82

You are now in a position to include the stakeholders for income sources 1 and 2, and the contributions of £100,000 and £3,000 in Example 2, or £56,000 and £47,000 in Example 3, can be entered in the input column on the Impact Map.

4 Note on capital or loan-financed projects

This is an area in which the SROI Network will be developing further guidance.

Where the investment is for an asset that will have a long life expectancy, such as a building, the calculation of the social return is more complex. It is made more complex still if the investment is financed by a loan.

Firstly, a building may have a life expectancy of many years and the activity in the building will generate value each year – a value that may itself last for more than one year. The value created depends, however, on the activities that happen in the building: activities that can only be supported by additional regular income.

Secondly, in the case of a loan, repayments over the period of the loan offset the investment in the first year. The only net cash flows over the life of the loan are the interest payments on the loan.

Currently, the guidance for using SROI in these situations is to focus on one year only and to emphasise that the SROI only examines the social value created by inputs that were necessary for the activity in that one year. Again, it may be helpful to involve your accountant here, if you have one.

In the case of a building, the inputs would be the costs of the activity, as discussed above, plus the depreciation for one year of the expected life of the building. There are accounting conventions for the life of buildings and your accounts will state what these are. This represents an allocation of the cost of the building to the overall costs that are required for the activities in the building.

5 Sources of support and further information

General

There are a number of online tools that are available to help you with SROI.
For more information go to the SROI network website:
www.thesroinetwork.org

nef has been working on SROI since 2001 and has pioneered its use in public policy.
For more information go to:
www.neweconomics.org

For an overview of evaluation in the voluntary sector, see *Practical Monitoring and Evaluation: a guide for voluntary organisations*, by Jean Ellis:
www.ces-vol.org.uk/index.cfm?pg=140

There is also information on many of the issues covered in this guide at:
www.proveandimprove.org

There are a number of tools on, including ones for full cost recovery, at:
www.philanthropycapital.org

For guidance on the economic assessment of spending and investment, and for related guidance, including the preparation of business cases for the public sector, see:
www.hm-treasury.gov.uk/data_greenbook_index.htm

To learn more about social accounting and social audit, see the SAN *Social Accounting and Audit Workbook*, Social Audit Network:
www.socialauditnetwork.org.uk

Really Telling Accounts!, by John Pearce and Alan Kay, can be found at:
www.socialauditnetwork.org.uk

Materiality

A number of reports relating to AccountAbility's work on redefining materiality can be found at:
www.accountability21.net

There is also a useful discussion of materiality in nef's report Investing in Social Value, which is available at:
www.thesroinetwork.org

Stage 1: Establishing scope and identifying stakeholders
Stakeholder involvement
Lots of information on engaging with people can be found at:
www.peopleandparticipation.net/display/Involve/Home

Participation Works! is available from:
www.neweconomics.org

AccountAbility has also produced a standard and a manual on stakeholder engagement, both of which are available from its website:
www.accountability21.net

Stage 2: Mapping outcomes
Cost analysis
A guide and a toolkit on cost allocation are available from ACEVO at:
www.acevo.org.uk/index.cfm/display_page/FCR_3rdsec_tools

Valuing inputs
Further information on valuing inputs is available at these three websites:
www.esf.gov.uk/_docs/July2006Rules_regs_-_Match_funding_trac.doc

www.volunteering.org.uk/NR/rdonlyres/0F4C3354-82C4-4306-907D-FBC31DCD0B04/0/ Calculatingvolunteervalue.pdf

www.statistics.gov.uk/pdfdir/ashe1108.pdf

Details of how to value goods in kind can be found at:
www.wefo.wales.gov.uk/resource/Annex%20C%20-%20Guidance%20note%20on%20 Match%20Funding%20in%20Kind%20February%2020073414.pdf

Stage 3: Evidencing outcomes and giving them a value
Sampling
Creative Research Systems provides information on sample design at:
www.surveysystem.com

Mapping outcomes and indicators
The Charities Evaluation Services website contains a range of resources on outcomes assessment in the voluntary sector:
www.ces-vol.org.uk

The Urban Institute's Center on Non-profits and Philanthropy has developed an outcomes framework for non-profit organisations. The framework has example outcomes and indicators for many different areas of activity:
www.urban.org

The website Homeless Outcomes is dedicated to resources for assessing outcomes in the homelessness sector, but the resources within, including Outcomes Star, are applicable to many organisations in the voluntary sector:
www.homelessoutcomes.org.uk

The following publications give guidance on outcomes assessment and outcomes tools:

Managing Outcomes: a guide for homelessness organisations, by Sara Burns and Sally Cupitt:
www.ces-vol.org.uk/index.cfm?pg=171

Your Project and its Outcomes, by Sally Cupitt:
www.ces-vol.org.uk/index.cfm?pg=165

Review of Outcomes Tools for Homelessness Sector, Triangle Consulting:
**www.homelessoutcomes.org.uk/resources/1/PDFsguidetotool/
ReviewofOutcomesTools.pdf**

Indicator databank
An indicator bank is being developed by the SROI Project supported by the Scottish Government.

Valuation
These websites provide more information on approaches to non-market valuation:
www.csc.noaa.gov/mpass/tools_nonmarket.html

www.ecosystemvaluation.org/contingent_valuation.htm

www.fao.org/DOCREP/003/X8955E/X8955E00.htm

HM Treasury (2003) *Green Book*:
www.hm-treasury.gov.uk/data_greenbook_index.htm

The following publications focus on valuing social goods:
Measuring the Value of Culture, Snowball J, Springer Verlag, Heidelberg DE, 2008.
A Primer on Nonmarket Valuation, Champ, Boyle and Brown, Kluwer, Dordrecht NL, 2003.

Using Surveys to Value Public Goods; the Contingent Valuation Method, Carson and Mitchell, Washington, USA, 1989.

Stage 4: Establishing impact
Deadweight
English Partnerships' Additionality Guide is available at:
www.englishpartnerships.co.uk/communitiespublications.htm

Stage 5: Calculating SROI
There are a number of case studies on the SROI Network website which include examples of how SROI has been calculated:
www.thesroinetwork.org

Stage 6: Reporting, using and embedding
Assurance
For more information on the options for the assurance of your report go to:
www.thesroinetwork.org

Other
Procurement
nef and the London Borough of Camden jointly developed an outcomes-focused
commissioning model based on SROI principles. Further details of the Sustainable
Commissioning Model can be found on the Sustainable Procurement website:
www.procurementcupboard.org

6 Downloads

Documents available from **www.thesroinetwork.org** include:
The guide (in full and in sections)
A blank Impact Map
The checklist
Further examples of Impact Maps
An example of an SROI report based on the worked example

7 A summary of the relationship between SROI and other approaches

Cost-benefit analysis
One difference between SROI and economic appraisal as described in HM Treasury's
Green Book is that SROI is designed as a practical management tool that can be used
by both small and large organisations, rather than from a macro perspective. SROI
focuses on, and emphasises, the need to measure value from the bottom up, including
the perspective of different stakeholders, while the Green Book appraisal is about
valuing costs and benefits to the whole of UK society. The main similarity between
SROI and the Green Book is that they both use money as a proxy of costs and benefits
arising from an investment, activity or policy.

Social accounting
Both SROI and social accounting are approaches used to measure the creation of
social value. SROI focuses on the perspective of change that is expected or happens
to different stakeholders as a result of an activity. Social accounting starts from an
organisation's stated social objectives. SROI and social accounting share a number of
common principles but social accounting does not advocate the use of financial proxies
and a 'return' ratio. SROI and social accounting can be compatible: the completion of
an SROI report is much easier if it is built on the basis of a good set of social accounts,
for example.

Outcomes approaches

The process of measuring outcomes as part of a theory of change is common to other outcomes models, such as that used by Charities Evaluation Services. The involvement of stakeholders is also a key feature of SROI that is emphasised, to a greater or lesser extent, in other outcomes models. The main difference between SROI and many other outcomes approaches is the importance of giving financial value to their outcomes.

The common ground between the initial stages of SROI and other outcomes approaches means that organisations that have already done a lot of work on outcomes are likely to find undertaking an SROI analysis much easier than organisations looking at outcomes for the first time.

Sustainability reporting

SROI shares basic principles, such as the importance of engaging with stakeholders, with approaches like the Global Reporting Initiative and AccountAbility's AA1000 standards.[1] SROI differs in that it develops simple theories of change in relation to significant changes experienced by stakeholders and includes financial proxies for the value of those impacts.

Other methods of economic appraisal

SROI is similar to other economic analyses that attempt to value and compare the costs and benefits of different kinds of activities that are not reflected in the prices we pay. This approach is particularly well developed in environmental economics.

Environmental impact assessment (EIA)

EIA is a methodology for assessing a project's likely significant environmental effects. It enables environmental factors to be considered alongside economic or social factors. EIA has to be completed as part of planning consent for major projects, as defined by European Community legislation. Like SROI, the assessment of what is considered 'significant' is critical.

8   The seven principles of SROI

1 Involve stakeholders:
Inform what gets measured and how this is measured and valued by involving stakeholders.
Stakeholders are those people or organisations that experience change as a result of the activity and they will be best placed to describe the change. This principle means that stakeholders need to be identified and then involved in consultation throughout the analysis, in order that the value, and the way that it is measured, is informed by those affected by or who affect the activity.

standards, the AA1000 Series, are principles-based standards that provide the basis for improving the erformance of organisations. They are applicable to organisations in any sector, including the public sector and any size and in any region.

ocial Return on Investment

2 **Understand what changes:**
Articulate how change is created and evaluate this through evidence gathered, recognising positive and negative changes as well as those that are intended and unintended.
Value is created for or by different stakeholders as a result of different types of change; changes that the stakeholders intend and do not intend, as well as changes that are positive and negative. This principle requires the theory of how these changes are created to be stated and supported by evidence. These changes are the outcomes of the activity, made possible by the contributions of stakeholders, and often thought of as social, economic or environmental outcomes. It is these outcomes that should be measured in order to provide evidence that the change has taken place.

3 **Value the things that matter:**
Use financial proxies in order that the value of the outcomes can be recognised. Many outcomes are not traded in markets and as a result their value is not recognised.
Financial proxies should be used in order to recognise the value of these outcomes and to give a voice to those excluded from markets but who are affected by activities. This will influence the existing balance of power between different stakeholders.

4 **Only include what is material:**
Determine what information and evidence must be included in the accounts to give a true and fair picture, such that stakeholders can draw reasonable conclusions about impact.
This principle requires an assessment of whether a person would make a different decision about the activity if a particular piece of information were excluded. This covers decisions about which stakeholders experience significant change, as well as the information about the outcomes. Deciding what is material requires reference to the organisation's own policies, its peers, societal norms, and short-term financial impacts. External assurance becomes important in order to give those using the account comfort that material issues have been included.

5 **Do not over-claim:**
Only claim the value that organisations are responsible for creating.
This principle requires reference to trends and benchmarks to help assess the change caused by the activity, as opposed to other factors, and to take account of what would have happened anyway. It also requires consideration of the contribution of other people or organisations to the reported outcomes in order to match the contributions to the outcomes.

6 Be transparent:

Demonstrate the basis on which the analysis may be considered accurate and honest, and show that it will be reported to and discussed with stakeholders.

This principle requires that each decision relating to stakeholders, outcomes, indicators and benchmarks; the sources and methods of information collection; the difference scenarios considered and the communication of the results to stakeholders, should be explained and documented. This will include an account of how those responsible for the activity will change the activity as a result of the analysis. The analysis will be more credible when the reasons for the decisions are transparent.

7 Verify the result:

Ensure appropriate independent assurance.

Although an SROI analysis provides the opportunity for a more complete understanding of the value being created by an activity, it inevitably involves subjectivity. Appropriate independent assurance is required to help stakeholders assess whether or not the decisions made by those responsible for the analysis were reasonable.

9 Checklist for SROI analysis

This is for your own use, to check your progress as you work through the guide.
For more information on the assurance process, go to: www.thesroinetwork.org

Checklist	Complete?
Stage 1: Establishing scope and identifying stakeholders	
Have you provided background information on the organisation?	
Have you explained why you are carrying out the analysis and for whom, including considering how you will communicate with them?	
Have you decided if you are analysing part of the organisation or all of it?	
Have you decided if you are analysing the social return in relation to a specific source of income or for activities funded by a number of sources?	
Have you decided whether this is an evaluation of the past or a forecast of the future?	
Have you decided what timescale to cover?	
Have you identified the resources you need (eg sufficient time, resources and skills)?	
Have you drafted a list of your stakeholders and completed the stakeholder table?	
Have you considered that some of these changes may happen to stakeholders that are outside your scope and whether you should revise the scope to include them?	
Stage 2: Mapping outcomes	
Have you completed the first two columns of the Impact Map for stakeholders and what you think happens to them?	
Have you documented your decisions on which stakeholders are material?	
Have you involved stakeholders in completing the next sections?	
For each stakeholder, have you included their contribution (input) to the activity (there may be some stakeholders that do not make an input)?	
Have you given the inputs a value?	
Have you checked to make sure that the inputs you have recorded include whole costs of delivering the service (eg overheads, rent)?	
Have you identified the inputs and outputs for the stakeholders?	

Have you included a description of the outcomes?	
Have you included intended and unintended changes?	
Have you included positive and negative changes?	
Have you completed the columns on the impact map for inputs, outputs and outcomes?	
At this point, do you want to add or remove stakeholders or stakeholder groups?	
Stage 3: Evidencing outcomes and giving them a value	
Have you identified indicators for the outcomes?	
How long do the outcomes last?	
Do you already have information in relation to each indicator?	
If not, do you have a plan for how you will gain this information?	
Have you completed the column for the source of the information?	
Have you completed the column for each indicator?	
For each outcome where you have not recorded one or more indicators, have you included the reason in your report?	
Can you record or forecast the amount of change in relation to each indicator?	
Have you identified a financial proxy for each outcome?	
Have you completed the column for the financial proxy?	
Have you completed the column for the source of the proxy?	
Are there any indicators for which you have not recorded a financial proxy? Have you included these in your report?	
Stage 4: Establishing impact	
Do you have information for deadweight in relation to each outcome?	
Do you think any of your estimates for deadweight can be explained by reference to displacement or attribution?	
If some deadweight can be explained by displacement, have you decided to add a new stakeholder (and/or change the scope)?	
If there is attribution, does this mean that you have missed out contributions made by other stakeholders who should now be added?	
Have you estimated attribution and recorded how you made the estimate?	

If the outcomes last for more than one time period, what happens to the outcome over this time period (drop-off)?	
Have you calculated impact (indicator multiplied by financial proxy minus percentages for deadweight, displacement and attribution)?	
Have you calculated any drop-off?	
As a result, are there any changes where the activity(ies) in the scope do NOT contribute to a significant change?	
Have you completed the columns for deadweight, attribution, displacement and drop-off?	
Stage 5: Calculating the SROI	
Have you set out the financial values of the indicators for each time period?	
Have you selected a discount rate?	
Do you have a total value for the inputs?	
Have you calculated: a) social return ratio, b) net social return ratio, c) payback period?	
Have you checked the sensitivity of your result for amounts of change, financial proxies, and measures of additionality?	
Stage 6: Reporting, using and embedding	
Have you summarised the changes required to the organisation's systems, governance or activities in order to improve ability to account for and manage social value created?	
Have you prepared a plan for these changes?	
Have you planned how to communicate your value in formats that meet your audiences' needs?	
If you have decided to produce a full report, does it include an audit trail of all decision-making, assumptions and sources?	
If you have decided to produce a full report, have you included a qualitative discussion of the assumptions and limitations underlying your analysis?	
Have you reviewed whether your communications created the desired effect in your audiences, and whether they liked the content and format?	
Have you decided on your approach to verification?	

	Wheels-to-Meals
	Provide luncheon club for 30 elderly local residents with additional health and social benefits by bringing residents to meals

Scope	Activity	30 places for eligible elderly and/or disabled local residents 5 days a week, 50 weeks of the year
	Contract/Funding/Part of organisation	Local Authority Grant

Stage 1 ➔ | **Stage 2 ➔**

Stakeholders	Intended/unintended changes	Inputs		Outputs	The Outcomes
		Description	Value £	Summary of activity in numbers	Description
Who do we have an effect on? Who has an effect on us?	What do you think will change for them?	What do they invest?			How would you describe the change?
elderly / disabled residents	residents use health services less	time	£0	luncheon club:	the mild/therapeutic group exercise sessions made residents fitter, they had fewer falls and ended up in hospital less
					the GP practise nurse group sessions helped residents manage their health and symptoms better and they were healthier
				– group activities (board games, craft, mild/ therapeutic exercise, info and awareness sessions)	residents made new friends and spent more time with others through the group activities
	residents get out of the house more				residents had nutritious meals with 3 (out of) 5-a-day and they were healthier
local authority	residents provided with nutritious meal	meals on wheels contract (annual)	£24,375		material outcomes for residents only (not for council). All outcomes for this stakeholder already considered above.
Wheels-to-Meals volunteers (retired)	keep active	time (at min wage) 4 volunteers x 3 hrs x 5 days x 50 wks x £6 (forecast)	£18,000	– transport for 30 people	healthier volunteers (retired)
neighbours of elderly/ disabled residents	look out for neighbours	time	£0	– 7500 hot meals annually	reduction in neighbourly care/shopping and break-down of informal community networks
Total			£42,375		

Name	
Date	

Objective of Activity		Time Period	1 year (2010)
Purpose of Analysis		Forecast or Evaluation	Forecast

Stage 3 ➡

The Outcomes (what changes)

Indicator	Source	Quantity	Duration	Financial proxy	Value £	Source
How would you measure it?	Where did you get the information from?	How much change was there?	How long does it last?	What proxy would you use to value the change?	What is the value of the change?	Where did you get the information from?
fewer falls and associated hospital admissions/stays annually	oneoff research	7	1 year	accident&emergency	£94.00	NHS cost book 07/08
			1 year	geriatric assessment inpatient	£4,964.00	
			1 year	geriatric continuing care-Inpatient (average 5 wks x £1,444)	£7,220.00	
fewer GP visits annually (appointments) and residents report improvement in physical health	questionaire and interviews	90	5 years	GP consultation	£19.00	NHS cost book 2006
new clubs/group activities joined during year and residents report an increase in personal wellbeing/ feeling less isolated	questionaire	16	1 year	average annual membership/cost	£48.25	current average costs of bus trips, bingo and craft clubs
fewer District Nurse visits and residents reporting increased physical activity of 3 hours or more a week	questionaire	14	2 years	District Nurse visits	£34.00	NHS cost book 07/08
volunteers report increased physical activity of 3 hours or more a week since volunteering	volunteer annual assessment	4	1 year	annual elderly residents swimming pass	£162.50	local authority
fewer instances of neighbours shopping for residents annually	One-off survey	275	3 years	supermarket online shopping delivery fee	- £5.00	www.tesco.co.uk

xt page)

	Wheels-to-Meals
	Provide luncheon club for 30 elderly local residents with additional health and social benefits by bringing residents to meals

Scope	Activity	30 places for eligible elderly and/or disabled local residents 5 days a week, 50 weeks of the year
	Contract/Funding/Part of organisation	Local Authority Grant

Stage 1 duplicate / **Stage 2 duplicate** / **Stage 4** ➡

Stakeholders	The outcomes	Deadweight	Attribution	Drop Off	Impact
	Description	%	%	%	
Groups of people that change as a result of the activity	How would you describe the change?	What would have happened without the activity?	Who else contibuted to the change?	Does the outcome drop off in future years?	Quantity times financial proxy, less deadweight, displacement and attribution
elderly / disabled residents	the mild/therapeutic group exercise sessions made residents fitter, they had fewer falls and ended up in hospital less	0%	5%	50%	£625.10
					£33,010.60
					£48,013.00
	the GP practise nurse group sessions helped residents manage their health and symptoms better and they were healthier	0%	10%	10%	£1,539.00
	residents made new friends and spent more time with others through the group activities	10%	35%	0%	£451.62
	residents had nutritious meals with 3 (out of) 5-a-day and they were healthier	100%	0%	0%	£0.00
local authority	material outcomes for residents only (not for council). All outcomes for this stakeholder already considered above.				£0.00
Wheels-to-Meals volunteers (retired)	healthier volunteers (retired)	70%	10%	35%	£175.50
neighbours of elderly/ disabled residents	reduction in neighbourly care/shopping and breakdown of informal community networks	5%	0%	5%	-£1,306.25
Total					£82,508.57

	Name				
	Date				
Objective of Activity		**Time Period**		1 year (2010)	
Purpose of Analysis		**Forecast or Evaluation**		Forecast	

Stage 5

Calculating Social Return

	Discount rate (%)		3.5%		
	Year 1 (after activity)	**Year 2**	**Year 3**	**Year 4**	**Year 5**
	£625.10	£0.00	£0.00	£0.00	£0.00
	£33,010.60	£0.00	£0.00	£0.00	£0.00
	£48,013.00	£0.00	£0.00	£0.00	£0.00
	£1,539.00	£1,385.10	£1,246.59	£1,121.93	£1,009.74
	£451.62	£0.00	£0.00	£0.00	£0.00
	£0.00	£0.00	£0.00	£0.00	£0.00
	£0.00	£0.00	£0.00	£0.00	£0.00
	£175.50	£0.00	£0.00	£0.00	£0.00
	-£1,306.25	-£1,240.94	-£1,178.89	£0.00	£0.00
	£82,508.57	£144.16	£67.70	£1,121.93	£1,009.74
Present Value*	£79,718.43	£134.58	£61.06	£977.70	£850.17
Total Present Value (PV)					£81,741.93
Net Present Value					£39,366.93
Social Return £ per £					£1.93: £1